THE IMPACT OF INFLUENCE VOLUME 5

Using Your Influence To Create A Life Of Impact

By
Chip Baker

Co-authored by Powerful Influencers

2022

THE IMPACT OF INFLUENCE

USING YOUR INFLUENCE TO CREATE A LIFE OF IMPACT

VOLUME 5

WRITTEN BY

CHIP BAKER

CO-AUTHORED BY POWERFUL INFLUENCERS

Copyright © 2022 by Chip Baker

All rights reserved. This book or any portion thereof may not be reproduced or used in any manner whatsoever without the express written permission of the publisher except for the use of brief quotations in a book review or scholarly journal.

First Printing: 2022

ISBN: 978-1-7379501-7-2

Ordering Information:

Special discounts are available on quantity purchases by corporations, associations, educators, and others. For details, contact the publisher at the email listed below.

U.S. trade bookstores and wholesalers:
Please contact chipbakertsc@gmail.com.

DEDICATION

This book is dedicated to all the people who have impacted our lives. We send a special dedication to our families and everyone who supports us. We hope that this book will leave an everlasting impact and influence many generations to come.

We are grateful for you!

To Bob, I hope this book inspires you. So good meeting today"

[signature]

PREFACE

Dear reader,

We hope that this book will be a blessing to you. In the following chapters, you will find the lessons that these powerful authors have learned throughout their journey to success. Our hope is that you will learn from these lessons and use them to help you operate more efficiently and effectively in your life.

Brief Description of Book

The Impact of Influence Vol. 5, Using Your Influence to Create a Life of Impact is overflowing with wisdom from visionary author, Chip Baker, and other powerful influencers who have discovered their paths to success. They are influencing many and impacting generations. The inspirational stories within the pages of this book will inspire you to make a positive difference for those around you.

TABLE OF CONTENTS

DEDICATION v
PREFACE vi
LIST OF AUTHORS IN CHAPTER ORDER 1
INFLUENCE IS LOVING THE PROCESS 2
RISE UP! 10
LOSER TO LEADER-WORDS MATTER 20
FIRST REAL INFLUENCE 28
HATTIE SUE 38
THE INFLUENCER 46
TURNING NEGATIVES INTO IMPACTFUL POSITIVES 54
LESSONS FROM THE COTTON FIELDS! 60
DAMAGED GOODS: FINDING BEAUTY IN THE JOURNEY 68
A DREAM BACKED BY HARD WORK 74
OUR JOURNEY TO VICTORY 82
MY ISLAND 90
DREAM IT, DO IT 100
THE IMPACT OF LANGUAGE 108
A LIFE-DEFINING MOMENT 118
WILL IT TO BE 128
GRIEF TO GREATER 136
THE POWER OF ONE 144
ABOUT THE LEAD AUTHOR 152
PICK UP THESE OTHER TITLES BY CHIP BAKER 154

LIST OF AUTHORS IN CHAPTER ORDER

1. Chip Baker
2. Bruce Villarreal
3. Carlton L. Todd
4. Charles Woods
5. Derrick Pearson
6. Jennifer Perez Solar
7. Jessica Perez
8. Johnny Martinez-Carroll
9. Jordon Lewis
10. Jose Escobar
11. Joshua Ogunyemi
12. Dr. Lindsie O'Neill Almquist
13. Megan Marie Randall
14. Melahni Ake
15. Petra Krebbs
16. R-Jay Barsh
17. TaMeka Martin
18. Victor Pisano

INFLUENCE IS LOVING THE PROCESS
Chip Baker

"The ultimate measure of a man is not where he stands in times of comfort and conveniences, but where he stands at times of challenge and controversy."
Martin Luther King Jr.

I have been blessed to be around some very influential people throughout my life. They impacted me and caused me to be who I am today. Those influential people in my life understood that the process to influence and impact was important. They seemed to love and enjoy that process. It was exhibited by the grace and elegance they showed to me and others that were fortunate to be around them.

"A plant needs time to take root and come to maturity, and the process cannot be hurried. The seedling must take root downward before it can bear fruit upward."
J. Oswald Sanders

Like a plant, they knew that the people they influenced needed that quality time to take root and come to maturity. They knew that to bear fruit we needed to be deeply rooted. Having a deeply rooted foundation allowed us to stand firm and hold on to our beliefs. They understood that it did not just happen over a short period of time. There was a process. Those influencers were deeply rooted, they had a firm foundation and they fell in love with the "Process".

People

The people that have influenced me valued people. They treated people the right way, regardless of what they felt the people could or could not offer them. They exhibited the Golden Rule which is "treat people how you want to be treated." They put themselves around the right people so they would have continued growth. They knew they were the sum total of the five people they hung around. Things are good and all, but people are important.

Relationships

"Life moves at the speed of our relationships."
Pastor Danny Green

Quality relationships are crucial. Relationships are the master key that opens the door to ongoing joy, fulfillment, influence, and impact. They had amazing relationships with people that were intentional about making a difference in the world. They could call on them at any time for help or advice and they would be there in a heartbeat. It was that way because their relationships were mutualistic. They gave and received quality in their relationships. It consisted of a listening ear, a shoulder to cry on, a hand to guide, a hug, and a huge smile. A smile transcends all barriers. It was mutualistic.

They understood that the most important relationship they had was the relationship with themselves. They knew that in order to give quality they had to be of substance. This means that they stood for something and had core common principles in which they lived out daily.

Obstacles

"The obstacle is the way."
Ryan Holiday

Their mindset about how they approached obstacles they faced was phenomenal. The influencers realized that the obstacle is the way and they loved attacking the challenges. Tough times taught them valuable lessons that helped them leave an impact later in life. A perfect example of this is in weightlifting. The weight is the obstacle. One must work on moving the "resistance" to become stronger. By getting more reps at moving the resistance or obstacle one becomes stronger. All things in life are that way. The obstacle is the way.

Commitment

The people that influenced and impacted me were committed. They were committed to making a difference and were inspiring to anyone that encountered them. The analogy I would like to share is the bacon and egg situation. The egg came from the chicken. The chicken laid the egg and went on about her business. The bacon came from the pig. The pig had to be sacrificed to have the bacon. THE PIG WAS COMMITTED!

The people that made a difference in my life were dang committed! They gave their all to everything they were involved in, or they did not waste their time doing it. They were committed to what they said they were going to do long after the feeling of excitement left them.

Experiences

"Reps make you better."
Chip Baker

Those great people understood the "Experience to Impact Cycle." It is a cycle that stems from valuing each experience we are blessed to have.

Experience brings knowledge.
Knowledge allows us to learn.
Applying what we learn lets us influence others.
Influencing others makes an everlasting impact.

This cycle is a must have and must be repeated to maximize our experiences. Reps make us better. It is within those quality reps where we gain the knowledge needed to influence and impact.

Sacrifices

"Advancement = Sacrifices"
Chip Baker

To have any type of significant advancement one must make sacrifices. In order to accomplish things we have not done before, we have to do things we have not done before. The people that influenced me made sacrifices. They always kept the main thing the main thing. My mother was a great example that sticks out to me. She was always focused on what was important. She worked multiple jobs to make sure the ends were met in our house. She took care of us well and did not let outside distractions deter her from accomplishing many great things. Despite tough circumstances she made sacrifices that propelled her to higher heights. It was awesome to see her accomplish all the things she did. She was the first to achieve many of those accomplishments or was groundbreaking with endeavors that impacted the lives of many. I still hear stories from people about her to this day.

Self-Care

"Self-care is not selfish."
Chip Baker

Growing up I was very involved. I was an athlete. At our house we used the old milk jugs as water jugs. After a long hard day, it was great to get home and drink a cold glass of water from the jug. I remember seeing the frost from the coldness as I would pour it in my cup. Once I drank the cold thirst-quenching cup of water, I was refreshed. It would allow me to recharge and move on to my next productive action.

This analogy explains how self-care works. We cannot pour out of an empty cup. The water represents self-care in our lives. After becoming exhausted and run down the water/self-care refreshes us and allows us to be great for others. Self-care is not selfish. Self-care gives us the fuel and energy to keep pushing. The process of valuing self-care allows us all to influence and impact others just like the amazing people I have been blessed to have in my life.

"Fall in love with the process of influencing and impacting."
Chip Baker

Influencing and impacting is important. Influencing and impacting requires a process. We must be aware of that process to make an everlasting impact. We must also fall in love with the PROCESS. People, Relationships, Obstacles, Commitment, Experiences, Sacrifices, and Self Care make up the process. God bless you on your journey! Go get it!

Fall in love with the PROCESS

People- Put yourself around good people. (We are the total of the 5 people we hang around most.)

Relationships- Life moves at the speed of our relationships.

Obstacles- The obstacle is the way. (Tough times teach us valuable lessons that will help us later in life.)

Commitment- Be committed to what you say you will do. (Bacon and Eggs, Pig and the Chicken)

Experiences- Experiences bring knowledge. (Knowledge is the key to success when used the right way.)

Sacrifices- Advancement equals sacrifice.

Self-Care- Take care of yourself. You cannot pour out of an empty cup.

ABOUT THE AUTHOR:

See Lead Author's Bio in About the Author section.

RISE UP!
Bruce Villarreal

"One of the Most Transcendental Life Experiences is when We RISE UP while going through Life's Fire and Life Pains. If we understand things happen FOR US, not to us, We Learn, Grow, and Transform. Creating our Life Masterpiece!"
-Bruce Villarreal

Pain

In life, after experiencing any kind of pain, whether it be Emotional or Physical, we don't want to hear or speak of such a word. What is Pain? Pain is a signal in your nervous system that something may be wrong. It is an unpleasant feeling, such as a prick, tingle, sting, burn, or ache. Pain may be sharp or dull. It may be intermittent, or it may be constant. Wow! What a definition! It makes my body shiver, shake, and ache just thinking about it. Who enjoys physical or emotional pain? No One! There are many life stories and life situations that we have all lived and survived. Some hurt more than others. Some leave emotional or physical scars. If we learn from them, use these life experiences to push us through to the next life level, or use them to encourage and empower others, they served their purpose. Life's pain can help us to WAKE UP! How many of us had our life awakening thanks to one of Life's painful experiences? That's when pain can turn into a blessing. As Steve Harvey (Comedian, Entrepreneur & Wealth Magnate) says: "Life happens for you, not to you!"

Different people have experienced life's pain at different stages of their lives. I admire and love to hear all the different types of *Successful Life Pain Survivors* and *Life Thriver Stories*. If you share yours instead of hiding it from others, that story can save someone's life. It can also inspire and encourage many people. It may just change one life. One life changed, transformed, or saved is priceless. It may positively affect many generations to come.

We all have the power to transform pain into victory. It does take introspection to self-analyze and see the lessons learned from those painful experiences. What do I mean, "*THANKS*" to those painful experiences? One of the lessons I've had to learn is to be grateful for what I have and count my blessings. There is always something to be grateful for when you're down, alone, broke, broken, sick, or confused. What can you be grateful for right now?

I too have had my life journey dealing with pain. Sometimes having a good fortunate life can lead someone to lose sight of the value of our life treasures, resources, gifts, and life privileges. Sometimes we have to lose it all to say, "Oh my God! What did I do?" or "What happened?"

Some have a rough start to life and learn gratitude early. They succeed later in life. Some succeed after losing it all. In my personal life, I was hit with the greatest pain ever … losing my marriage, family, business, and my Health.

Fire

Let's talk about fire. What does it mean literally and metaphorically? Fire is used to produce heat, light up, burn, destroy, or cleanse. Metaphorically, it can represent someone's passion, wrath, or destruction. In some cases, we have been the fire that warms someone's soul or being. We have been that light that motivated someone to tap into their passions. When we are pained by the Fires we create, for ourselves or by others, it hurts, burns and can pierce our soul. Fire can be powerful, cleansing, healing, or destructive. It can spark change, union, or even a revolution. We must learn to control the fire within us and learn to use it to benefit the world around us.

Let's talk about the pain caused by someone's uncontrolled fire or pain. This happens when they have unresolved traumas that can cause the burning of others, themselves, and those they love. It is important to acknowledge, seek healing, and help to calm this fire. When we heal, we heal others as well.

There's the fire that cleanses and purifies. When we are pained by the Fires we create for ourselves or by others Fire, ouch that hurts and can burn and pierce our souls. Isaiah 48:10 says, "Behold, I have refined You, but not as silver; I have tested you in the furnace of affliction." Life is a constant series of circumstances that, if viewed objectively, are designed to make us better, purify us, and make us *RISE UP!*

Rise Up

It can be challenging to Rise Up especially when we are down and in troubled circumstances. It's easy to give advice freely to others when we are happy, positive, and stress free. When it's time to use our own advice or wisdom of the great it seems like mere philosophy. Our faith, love, strength, and wisdom will be tested. Rising up, at times will require forgiving ourselves, asking for forgiveness, connecting with our source, and others. Rising up requires us to discipline our mind, heart and soul to push forward no matter the obstacles. In my past, I was very weak minded.

We can all Rise Up. We have to know that we can. Most of us have been mentally conditioned. It's important to educate ourselves and break free from our past mental conditioning. Some people think common sense is common. "Common sense is not common."

Some of us have been exposed to great mentors, business leaders, or life changing information. That's not enough. It's important for that information to be analyzed, internalized, and put into consistent practice. The inertia of our past schooling and habits will cause us to drift back. Rising up is a daily battle. It will require ten thousand hours of action and focus to master and eliminate any bad habits. You must replace them with daily discipline and action toward achieving your life purpose.

Learn

It's important to have a winner's mentality dedicated to learning. We don't lose or fail, we learn. We fail only if we don't learn. No one is perfect, but we can improve ourselves through self-awareness and constant self-analysis. There is always a lesson behind our painful life situations and circumstances. When you learn to ask yourself, "Hey what is Life or God trying to teach me?" When you are a conscious being you are constantly asking yourself what's the lesson behind each situation or circumstance. Learning is available to all of us for free. We can master any subject with focus and massive action. We have to repeat and practice until it becomes second nature. Also, seek out a mentor for the area you want to master. You will have many opinions by lots of people. They can even come from qualified mentors or books. Please remember that advice or information can sometimes be incorrect. We must learn to filter to find good information that will help you grow. We must use our intuition to decide what feels right.

Some people have their own agenda when counseling or guiding you. You have the final decision to what makes your heart happy. A mentor isn't perfect. We are all imperfect beings looking to evolve and transcend. A real mentor should be successful in the field they are mentoring you in. Specialized mentoring or knowledge is encouraged. We must be willing to invest in ourselves by hiring a coach, attending seminars, webinars, courses, or purchasing books like this one. You will leave with one life changing nugget or many. As an entrepreneur these books, seminars, and coaching are partially or fully tax deductible - take advantage of these perks. If you're not an entrepreneur or small business owner become one. If you need guidance or coaching in this matter reach out to me and I can help you.

Grow

I'm sure you have heard the expression, "Growing Pains."

If there is no pain, there is no gain. For growth to occur you will feel tension and be uncomfortable. Nobody likes to be in uncomfortable situations. I don't. I learned that to grow, heal or open new doors of opportunity life shakes us up or moves us around. Sometimes lightly and on other occasions rocks our world, but all for our greater good!

When Steve Harvey made the decision to drop his traditional job to go full time as a Comedian, he was homeless for 3 years living out of his vehicle. He lost it all. He recounts having to sleep in hotel parking lots, parks, and rest areas. He even had to fish with his fishing pole to get a meal. He said, "I lost it all."

This taught him to value everything and the important people in his life. He had a vision for himself, and this vision helped carry him through his growing pains. He learned to be a tough person when necessary. He says, "We are being processed by life and God." This is to bring out the greater version of you and us! If you're being shaken by life, going through life's growing pains a *Big Blessing* is coming your way. Knowing this changes how we see challenges. It helps us go from discouragement to encouragement and inspiration. Steve Harvey's twenty-dollar jokes now pay him millions!

Don't underestimate your potential, your temporary circumstance, and your personal vision. Focus on the promise, the greater good, and blessing that is coming your way! My youngest child, now a young man, Bruce Fernando Villarreal, is a great example for me and for many. He is on the Varsity Cheer squad at his High School. He has grown by qualifying to represent his school.

First, his grades had to be at top notch. Second, he practiced, mastered his routines, somersaults, and flips. Third, he has been disciplined with his diet and exercise to have a lean body that can perform. He is a beauty of a young man both internally and externally. He has been one of my Life Teachers. When he was three years of age, he told me his million-dollar quote, "Dad I can make anything from nothing." I'm proud of you Son and am honored to be your father!

Transform

The definition of Transformation: a dramatic change in form or appearance, metamorphosis, an induced or spontaneous change. Words that have to do with Transformation:
- Change
- Alteration
- Modification
- Transfiguration
- Evolution
- Reconstruction
- Rebuilding
- Reorganization
- Restyling
- Renewing
- Revamping
- Revolutionizing
- Metamorphosis
- Revolution
- Transmutation

I invite you to connect with the definition and the words describing transformation. Which one do you identify with? Which one best describes your current situation, your next step, or your vision? Transformation is inevitable to create the magic in your life and help you realize your dreams. If you transform then the positive effects are long lasting and generational. Commit to transform your life and create your life masterpiece.

Create Your Life Masterpiece

Speaking of art and creating a *Life Masterpiece*, my favorite artist is a beautiful young woman, Carolina "KAKO" Villarreal (My first-born Daughter), whom has had a passion for art since she was a little girl. At the age of 13, she recognized her calling as an artist. She has developed into a well-known artist, with museum exhibitions and national recognition. She also has a successful product and clothing line featuring her art designed by "PWR Couture" with Her Partner, Mentor and Mother, Vanessa Castillo. I'm proud of both of them!

Like a work of art, we can create our dream life, our *Life Masterpiece*. Even during difficult moments, it may seem like you are living a nightmare, but if that vision, purpose, or dream is clear, it will carry you through and past the difficult times until you reach your promised land. I love Steve Harvey's Success story because of how he turned his life around. He went through two divorces, was broke, and homeless. He now has his family life in order as well as his business life. He is now worth close to a billion dollars and going for more. He mentions that he had two hundred meetings to pitch his business ideas and out of those meetings only made five home runs. They only write about his five successful meetings, not the one hundred ninety-five meetings that were turned down. His family is now united and travels the world together. He is in a happy marriage and has become a great role model to emulate. If Steve Harvey was able to *Rise Up* despite the pains and fires of life and created a *Life Masterpiece*, so can we, so can You!

Life is beautiful. God is great. You are a miracle. Pray Daily. Stay grateful and remember, I believe in YOU, RISE UP!

I want to Thank and Honor My Top 3 Life teachers, mentors and sources of inspiration: My 2 Children, Beginning with my Daughter Carolina "Kako" Villarreal , The Artist and she is going Global. My Son Bruce Fernando Villarreal, The Varsity Cheer Leader, soon one of the Best Forensic Detectives. Vanessa Castillo, Mentor and Mother of our 2 Beautiful Children, Business Woman, and Founder of "PWR Couture." I want to extend My Eternal Love and Gratitude to all 3 for being with Me in the Good, the Bad and the Difficult.

-Bruce Villarreal

ABOUT THE AUTHOR:

Social Media:
IG @mrbvtheoriginal
FB @bruce.villarreal.5
Email bruce@mrbvglobalcompanies.com

Bruce Villarreal is originally from Hawthorne, California. In 1996 he moved to El Paso, Texas. El Paso is where his heart is and has been home for the last twenty-six years. He has been an entrepreneur since the tender age of thirteen when he was selling seafood by making cold calls for his Father's seafood business. His first major success was in network marketing with Herbalife International. While there, he was mentored by one of the MLM Legends (Founder Mark Hughes) and Jim Rohn, the Father of Personal Development.

His passion is public speaking. He has a gift for communicating and connecting with people. Bruce is a businessman, member of the prestigious "League of Business" (Entrepreneurial Business Organization), Co-Founder of the "Gentlemen of Business", and currently has several businesses. His businesses are in the following industries: Solar, Home Water Treatment Systems, Credit Repair, and Business Credit. He is Currently Building a Financial & Life Insurance Services Agency. Bruce is a self-development speaker and is now a Published Author.

LOSER TO LEADER-WORDS MATTER
Carlton L. Todd

"Not winning is never an option. How I will win is!"
-Dr. Carlton L. Todd

A leader with no power or influence is just a title. I did not find leadership; leadership found me. As far back as I can remember, I have always been a leader, even as a kid reared in the church. I was always placed in the forefront even when I didn't want to be. I was the multitalented kid that always found himself in the spotlight. Sometimes it was not because of my talent, but my personality. The effects of being thrust into settings I did not ask to be a part of caused me to explore and exploit boundaries. Add in adolescence. Now, think about that one kid that often tests your "inner gangster" as a parent or student...that was me!

I was a smart kid, very mouthy and always pushed the envelope. I was blessed to have natural charisma and a love for all people. As a kid, I could easily persuade my classmates to go along with my antics, foolishness, and mayhem. You see, I was a leader that used my influence to negatively impact others. I remember one day in the sixth grade, I told the class, "Today, we are not doing any work. But y'all got to have my back. Y'all know once I make her mad, she will go on a rant and before you know it, class will be over! Everybody got me?"

The whole class responded, "YES!"

Everybody bought in, including the good kids and the innocent ones too. Did I mention I was the ultimate class-clown?

Our teacher came in ready to teach. She said, "I'm going to give you all some time to get this done." As she walked around, I decided to go to work. I made noises to distract her and agitate her.

"Who is that? Todd is that you?" she asked in an accusatory tone.

"What? Why are you always picking on me?" I responded in a shocking voice.

"I'm watching you!" she replied.

"And I'm watching you!" I said sarcastically.

Time went on and I did it again. This time, she really flipped her lid.

At the top of her lungs, she yells out, "It's you! I saw you!" Her rant went on for about thirty minutes. By this time, class was up, and my mission was accomplished. She asked me to stay back so she could chat with me. The words she said to me changed my life forever!

"You are a loser! I dread coming to this place every day because I have to see you. One day, I'm going to read about all the things you did that will land you in prison. Loser! You won't even graduate from high school! Loser! Now, get out of my room. Loser!"

She uttered those words with complete disgust.

Now as troublesome as I was, those words hurt my feelings. Quite naturally, my job for the rest of the year was to make her life a living hell. I succeeded most days. If she said I was going to be a loser, then I was going to prove to her right. I proved her right because I was cheating myself and my classmates out of learning. I was proving her right because I almost fell into her narrative of me. Subconsciously, at that moment I wanted to be a teacher so I could be a better one than her. I wanted to be a principal, so I could get rid of all the teachers that made students feel like losers. I wanted to show her that she would one day regret her words.

The kid she labeled as a loser graduated high school as the Senior Class President. The kid she labeled as a loser went to college, became a teacher, then a principal, and received a Ph.D. I wanted her to know that the hell I gave her was the hell I would give myself every time I thought about quitting and giving up. I gave myself hell every time I considered the thought of a task as hard or impossible to complete. I gave myself hell until I reached all my goals simply because I refused to be a statistic, but most importantly I refused to be a loser!

As I reflect, it is my belief that leadership is an art and science. Leadership is an art when it comes naturally for some. When leadership is an art, it can be flawless, effortless, and come in the form of a gift. The art of leadership is not strenuous or forced. Leadership that is in the form of an art can blossom and work in any environment. Leadership in the form of an art can be rare but can prosper anywhere - it is universal! For example, there are people that are in prisons who are great leaders, yet their influence threatens others' safety. In every organization, there are informal leaders who do not carry the title but have the power. Leadership has authority, but not every leader has power.

When thinking about a specific leadership style, one must be intentional about how to perform to shape the culture and climate of the organization. This analysis of performance is a skill set that many do not possess. It takes the science of leadership to effectively implement specific characteristics to accommodate the needs. These attributes define how authority looks and how it is represented.

Authority states what I can and cannot do. Authority is compliance which indicates, "I'm only doing this because I'm expected to do so." Authority makes people follow policies, protocols, and procedures. Authority has a title and is often used to coerce its followers to submission. Power has followers that believe in the message, person, and cause. Power can encourage people to give up their personal time, talent, and treasure without expecting anything but an outcome. Power does not need a title but with a title it can be efficacious, innovative with limitless boundaries. Power has the buy in that authority does not. I often ask leaders, "What's more important, authority or power?"

I was taught at an early age that presentation was everything! Don't just look the part but be the part. I often refer to authority as looking the part and power to being the part. Too many times in leadership we focus on the look and not the work. We focus on the look and not the process it takes to really become excellent. Most importantly, we focus on the look and not the people. My belief is the people you lead are the most important piece to your success.

I became the leader I am today because of the leadership styles and behaviors I experienced throughout my life. Though there are many great leaders I have had the privilege to serve under, I am the leader I am today because of the poor leadership experience I personally encountered in my career. I remember the worst leader I ever had. It was a male principal whom I worked for around my seventh year in education. It was the first time in my career that I hated my job. This leader was self-serving, dismissive, condescending, underhanded, etc. and the list continues. This principal led with fear and intimidation. No one ever knew where they stood with him. There were times when unethical decisions were made.

This leadership triggered "Little Carlton the Loser." I questioned if I was "good enough." There was never praise, affirmation, nor appreciation for anything. I recall falling into a deep depression. I was okay and fine when I got up in the mornings preparing for work. I was even okay on my way to work. Whenever I would turn on the street of the school, that is when my stomach would drop, and my heart would begin to get heavy. Let me be clear, I loved my students and coworkers, but I hated everything else about that place. I developed such a loathing for that place that I became disgusted with the way it looked, smelled, and sounded.

I wanted out! I was miserable, I had anxiety and I always anticipated the worst. I was humiliated and berated in front of my peers. Again, remember up until that point in my career, I had great work experiences and excelled. Until that point, I never knew what it was like to hate the place you work. I remember feeling defeated, overwhelmed and "stuck." I remember this feeling as if it were yesterday. My prayer was, "I'm stuck, and I'm lost, and I know there must be greater for me. My gifts are not utilized for my purpose. My growth is stunted, and my voice is silent. I feel helpless and abandoned." I prayed and asked God for direction and clarity. Why was "HE" allowing this to happen to me? I wanted to understand the assignment and pass the test.

I immediately received the confirmation I was looking for. You see, I was so anxious to be promoted that I allowed myself to accept anything to fulfill my personal timeline aspirations. The truth is, I had not paid attention to all the red flags. I was blocked two times before I landed in that position. If I had been obedient to all the signs, I could have avoided this experience. Now, as I reflect it was necessary, because I had to experience what ineffective leadership looked like. I had to experience this so I would know what not to do as a leader.

In that moment, I vowed that I would never let an individual have that experience under my leadership. It was at that moment I understood Dr. Maya Angelou, when she stated, "People will forget what you said, people will forget what you did, but people will never forget how you made them feel." In that moment it solidified my understanding that it matters how you treat people. The words that you allow to leave your mouth and fall on others' ears matter. Your attention matters. Your investment in others' goals and opportunities matters. A happy environment where others feel safe and supported matters. I learned as a school administrator, a leader in my church and a leader in my community that these unwanted experiences are what keeps me humble, human, and hungry for new opportunities to expand my horizon while building confidence in the people I lead. These unwanted experiences developed my purpose, passion, and mission. I was created to motivate, encourage, and inspire. When you know your purpose, you know your destiny. These unwanted experiences are the reason I wake up every morning and say, "Not winning is never an option. How I will win is! Now let's win the day!"

ABOUT THE AUTHOR:

Social Media:
IG @carlton.todd.94
FB @carlton.todd.94
Email carlton_todd@yahoo.com

Dr. Carlton L. Todd was born and raised in Dallas, Texas. Todd is a product of the Dallas Independent School District, where he graduated from David W. Carter High School. His leadership skills were evident then as he was selected by his peers as Class President. Destined for greatness, Todd attended Prairie View A&M University where he received his Bachelors in Interdisciplinary Studies in Education with an emphasis in Reading. A Master's Degree in Education Administration and Curriculum & Instruction with an emphasis in Reading. Todd also received his Doctor of Philosophy in Education Leadership in 2016. His dissertation topic was The Impact of a Mentoring Program for African American Males in a Rural School District in Southeast Texas. Todd's research won first place in the 2016 Research Association for Minority Professors Conference. Todd is also a proud member of the oldest and coldest Alpha Phi Alpha Fraternity Incorporated.

Todd has served as a Junior High Reading and Language Arts Teacher, Instructional Coach, High School Testing Coordinator, and Assistant Principal. Todd currently serves in the role as a Junior High Principal. Todd is also the founder of the male mentoring organization, Boyz 2 Men, which has subgroups planted in several districts in the greater Houston area. Carlton is married to the love of his life, Shaikethia Jones Todd, and they have one daughter, Taylor, who is a student at the University of Texas in San Antonio. As a man of faith, Todd attributes his success and accomplishments to God. The young doctor and his family are active members in their church where Todd also serves as Minister of Music and as a Youth Ministry leader. Dr. Todd and his family resides in Cypress, Texas.

FIRST REAL INFLUENCE
Charles Woods

When you have siblings, it is an extraordinary situation. There can be bonds that are created unlike any other bonds that you will ever experience. I am blessed to be the brother of two older sisters. Bridgett is a little over a year older than me and Cat is nine years older. As a kid, Cat was my rock, my heart, and my soul. She spent a lot of time taking care of me and Bridgett. Some of that time was by choice, but most was mandated by my parents. No matter the reason, I could not tell the difference because Cat showed me and Bridgett nothing but love. Looking back, I cannot imagine how hard it was to be a teenage girl taking care of your younger sister and brother while not being afforded the opportunity to be a kid. She was not able to go certain places, or she would be charged with having us tag along. There is no doubt it was rough on Cat but the selfish side of me is extremely grateful for the moments that we spent together.

As an adolescent male, I was maturing while gaining a sense of mental and physical toughness/strength. Several people would say those traits are typically learned from your father, older brothers, or some sort of male figure. For me those traits were learned from my father and my oldest sister. My father taught me about using your hands and working hard. Cat taught me everything else. In an effort to make me a tough, self-sufficient young man plus stop me from crying so much, my sister would wrestle with me, show me how to play different sports, and inspire me with pep talks. She was one of the toughest individuals that I knew, physically and mentally. While in elementary school, Cat made sure I was not getting picked on or mistreated by older kids. I always felt like I was safe while I was with her. When I was not having a good day and my spirits were low, she knew exactly what to say and when to say it. She was motivating me before I knew anything about motivation. She made sure that I kept my head up and minimized those obstacles that might interfere with positive growth.

Cat always spoke the truth to me and answered my questions with no hesitation. She had a great heart even though her toughness did not come solely from a good place. Cat dealt with many different situations that most kids her age would not have been able to endure. She was involved in physical altercations with peers, there were a few issues with coaches, and at times there were issues between her and my parents.

As I got older, I gained a better understanding of why she played basketball and why she played so hard during her years on the team. This was her sanctuary, the place where she could be a kid. The place where she did not have any responsibility but to play the game and she could get all her frustration out. Those days that I got to see my sister play, I saw first-hand how physically and mentally tough she was. That was the same toughness that she wanted to ingrain in me.

Cat had the ability to take any situation that she was in and make the best of it. She held down a job, working late hours while also doing homework, going to basketball practice, and games. Cat also had to deal with playing time issues and my parents trying to be supportive but not making the situation better. That could create an awkward space for a child that just wants to play the game she loved.

This chapter of Cat's life taught me that it is my responsibility to ensure that I am physically and mentally tough enough to handle the obstacles that are placed in my path. I learned that hard work and recognizing where I am mentally will determine my abilities. It will also help me understand the amount of time it will take me to accomplish my goals. Strength is not only about lifting weights. Strength is also being an advocate for yourself, being able to say no to bad situations, being able to do the right thing even when the right thing may not be cool to the majority, and completing what you started. These are the types of strengths that were infused in me by the examples from my sister.

It was a happy time for my family. Cat had just graduated from high school. We were on our way to Ruston, Louisiana to drop her off at Gambling State University where she would be a student athlete, working on a college degree and playing college basketball. This would be my first time on a college campus, and I was extremely excited to share this experience with my sister. Once we arrived, we moved her belongings into her dorm room and took a tour of the campus. We stayed in Ruston a little longer than was planned but it was good to spend that time with Cat since she was going to be gone for a while. On our way back home, I was a little sad, but happy for her at the same time. My sister deserved this chance at her own life.

I believe it was about two or three weeks later and my sister returned home with all the items that we left with her in Ruston, Louisiana. I had no idea what was going on, but I knew something had changed, something was wrong. I knew she would come home to visit but this seemed different. About two days later Cat explained to me that she was not going back to college at this time. She had a new journey in life. My sister was going to be a mother and I was going to be an uncle. It was a sad but happy time for our family. I was sad to see my sister not be able to attend her college of choice playing basketball, but I was excited to be an uncle to my unborn nephew.

My parents could not offer my sister a whole lot of assistance and our living arrangements were not the best. Cat did not let those obstacles stop her from being her best. Not only the best for her as a future mother but also her best as a big sister. Cat kept a job and worked very hard to support her new family, plus me and Bridgett.

She helped my parents with bills until she got a place of her own. Cat faced an extreme amount of pressure and stress. She handled it with no complaints. It seemed as if it was easy for her, but remember that thought came from an adolescent that did not see everything that was taking place at that time. I admired my sister for her resilience and strength.

I have no choice but to be resilient. Cat was the poster board for resilience. I was able to witness first-hand how she overcame so many obstacles. She showed me that there is no place for giving up or feeling sorry for yourself.

"Brush yourself off and get back in the fight!!!" I will never forget a conversation Cat and I had one morning when she was dropping me off at school when I was in Junior High. I was going through a rough-time, and she knew it. She looked at me with a straight face before I got out of the car and with a stern voice she stated, "We are like Vikings. We can survive anything!!!" To most that statement would not mean a whole lot, but for me that was motivation. Those words meant the world to me and made me believe that nothing could stop us. We could make it through any trials and tribulation that we faced.

No matter what I was going through there was always one thing that I knew for certain. There was no doubt in my mind that my sister loved me. It felt like she loved me more than she loved herself at times. I do not remember Cat being mad, angry or annoyed by me as a kid. Even when I was her unofficial escort to places where she was going with her friends. When we went to the corner store, the park, activities at the junior high campus, and many other places; she never made me feel unwanted. Cat was unselfish when it came to me. If I asked for something she would get it for me, if she was able. Even when I did not ask, she would take it upon herself to treat me with things that she knew I liked.

Cat eventually moved to Huntsville with her family, her husband and son, to attend college at Sam Houston State University. Even during those times, she made sure that she supported me and Bridgett. Cat would pick us up from our parents' house on the weekends, so we could get away for a little while. She tried to move me in with her family on two different occasions, but that did not work. I knew that her love did not have anything to do with this not working, it just was not a good idea at that time.

My senior year of high school I moved in with Cat, my two nephews, and my soon to be niece. It was amazing to see the excitement that my sister had for me as I completed my senior year. She was excited that it was my senior year, and I was receiving offers to play college football, which gave me a chance to receive a college education.

Cat made it a huge deal that I had been nominated to be homecoming king. She made it a point to let me know that I would be the first black homecoming king in school history and when I won, WOW!!! She won also. She was so excited. I had to calm her down since she was about seven months pregnant with my niece. Cat was there with me when I signed my college scholarship and when I walked across the stage at my High School graduation.

These are just a few of the acts of love that my sister, Cat showed me. Most of these acts occurred in a time when the world was not so kind to her. It was phenomenal that Cat continued to love me unconditionally no matter what the world dished out.

Cat showed me how to be selfless and truly love. There were no strings attached with anything that she did. When she cared about you, she cared about you. I grew as a man with a caring heart and awareness of others because of what I learned from her. I owe my sister, Cat a lot of the credit for the person that I am today.

(S-R-L) Strength, Resilience and Love

The three main traits discussed in the above paragraphs were strength, resilience, and love. These traits were monumental in my sister's journey through life and extremely impactful in my life. Cat displayed these traits with no effort because these traits were a part of her authentic identity. I can only hope to do the same and impact others the same way she impacted me. Focusing on these three traits is a GREAT start to a positive journey through life.

- Make sure you are mentally and physically strong enough to take on any obstacles that present themselves. Take care of your mental space which helps to prepare you physically. Be grateful for the opportunity to work on your **STRENGTHS** and seek out support if support is needed. You never have to face your obstacles alone.
- **RESILIENCE** is about moving forward quickly when faced with difficulties. Do not waste time on the things that you cannot control. Focus on growth and the desire to be better. Better than you were one minute ago.
- Lead with positive energy and learn to **LOVE** and care for others. Focus on making life better for those around you or in your care. Caring for others does not take a lot of effort. Open your heart and allow yourself to be that relief for those in need.

Cat was not perfect, and I am far from perfect. The traits and life lessons that I acquired from my sister as we grew through life were some of the most valuable. Those lessons aided me in accomplishing my goals and becoming a better version of myself. Cat tested the waters of life and tackled life's difficulties so I would not have to experience those types of struggles. It is amazing how very few individuals realize the impact that someone has on their life until they take the time to reflect on past experiences. As I wrote this chapter, I realized that my sister, Cat, had the very first positive impact on my life. I cannot express the amount of gratitude that I have for her. I was fortunate to have her in my life and I am fortunate to have her as my sister.

You must determine what type of life you want to live and what type of impression you want to leave on others. These impressions may be intentional, or they may just happen. You do not have to be driven by the same (S-R-L) traits that were discussed above or even the same number of traits. My only hope for you is that you will leave an everlasting impression on others like Cat left an everlasting impression on me.

ABOUT THE AUTHOR:

Social Media:
IG @charleswoodsww
FB @charleswoodsww
Email woodzworxgroup@gmail.com

Charles has twenty plus years in public education, nine years as a classroom teacher and football coach, six years as a head boys track coach, five years as an assistant principal and this year makes his sixth year as a building principal.

Charles has a M.S. in Engineering and Technology Management and a B.S. in Industrial Technology from the University of Louisiana at Lafayette. He is a multiple time bestselling author for his collaborative work in The Winning Mindset, Black Men Love and The Impact Of Influence Volume 1, 2 and 4. Charles is a servant leader that takes pride in having a Positive Mindset and being a Mentor, Coach and Speaker.

Charles is married to his beautiful wife Celena Woods and has two daughters Courtney and Chelsea Greer.

His certifications include:
- EC-12 Superintendent Certification
- EC-12 Principal Certification
- EC-12 Special Education Certification
- Non-Crisis Intervention Trainer
- Rice University Leadership Partner's Executive Education Academy

"There is no other profession that gives me the opportunity to impact lives like public education. I did not choose this path; this path chose me. I will continue to be a servant leader to those in my care and for those that choose to work with me. I am forever grateful for this opportunity to make a difference in the lives of others. I live to serve, I do not serve to live!!!"

Quotes:

"Don't be a product of your environment, make your environment a product of a positive you!!!"

HATTIE SUE
Derrick Pearson

What is your name little boy?

It was one of thousands of questions asked and answered at the same time by one of the greatest influences over my life.

What is your name little boy?

It was the truth and the way. It was a statement of absolution. It was a question of purpose and intent. The woman who had ownership of these words was this beautiful powerhouse and North Star. She was absolute and a mystery. She was the most powerful force in the universe and the most caring sensitive soul I have ever known. She loved the loudest, proudest, and most often. She never feared because that would be disrespectful to her incredible faith. She was domestic and worldly, quiet but always heard, and was loved in return in the most absolute of ways. She was a giant of a woman standing at about five foot three or so. She could smile you into tears of joy and stare you down as if she were Medusa herself. Real goddess stuff.

The woman was Hattie Sue Keaton Harris. Hattie Sue. The matriarch. The Boss. My grandmother.

Born in Lunenburg, Virginia on July 28, 1911, daughter of William Keaton and India Rainey Keaton. She once told me her nickname was "Plue," but I never understood what it meant. It was not regal enough in my mind. We shared July 28th as both of our birthdays. There was always a special smile shared between us when the date rolled around. She would whisper that I was her 51st "Birthday present". It made me feel special that we shared that. She loved her gang of grandchildren all the same, but I had that special thing as my own.

My grandmother was a spiritual woman in full. Sunday mornings before church featured gospel from Reverend James Cleveland, The Staple Singers, or Mighty Clouds of Joy. Sunday mornings also featured an aroma that would best be described as what heaven must smell like. It was a combination of fried chicken, ham, pie, cookies, sweet potatoes, and love. I get tears just thinking about it. Cooking was a thing she loved to do for people she loved the most. Us. She would start on Saturday and roll through until those rolls or biscuits were ready. There is no greater memory or aroma than that.

In my early years, my grandmother lived a block away with her backyard overlooking my backyard. Whatever shenanigans were taking place or was about to take place was met with this super spy opening of her kitchen door or dining room window and this BOLD "DERRRRRRIIICCCKKK!" "Little boy!"

I even tried to practice not freezing up in full like a game of freeze tag when I heard it, but soon learned that it was easier and safer to just behave. The calling of the name was one thing, but it was this OTHER little thing that my grandmother had that is still the most powerful thing I know. My cousins and siblings will all vouch for this.

If someone was misbehaving, misspeaking, misunderstanding, or simply not making her proud, my grandmother would do this thing with her eyes and her lips. She would curl her lips back in as if she were biting on them. Then stare at you as if lightning bolts would shoot from her eyes. This was the sign that all things going on must cease IMMEDIATELY. IMMEDIATELY!

Whenever you saw this, you had a business decision to make. Were you willing to risk the opening of the sky and the earth at the same time? We learned better, sooner. The times when the lesson had to be learned, she was the world's best teacher. Even at 60, my grandmother was fast and quick. She could have been a pro wrestler, I am sure. She could cut you off at any corner of the dining room table, backyard, or basement couch. And she loved us all enough to make sure that that behavior never appeared again.

What is your name little boy?

When I was twelve, I moved in with my grandmother, great uncle, grandfather, and oldest sister Diane. I was there to help with little things like garbage and mowing the lawn. As I recall, I was mainly there to taste cake batter and icing. I would explain the sports I was watching on her television when I knew she would much rather be watching anything else and help with my grandfather. These were the days of not having a TV in every room, and there was only one phone line that everyone shared. I was just getting into girls. She was detailed in outlining the dos and don'ts of phone conversation, conversation length, and proper dismount from said calls.

What is your name little boy?

I was to introduce myself to whomever answered the phone. It was the price you pay for calling someone's home. Oddly, I was pretty good about it. Hello, Sir or Ma'am. My name is Derrick Pearson, and I would like to talk to your daughter. Like clockwork. I never asked why this was needed or important, it was simply enough because she said it was. Never once thought about it again. No need to ask. And then.

At age 13 I called the home of a young lady, and her father answered the phone. I said, "Good evening, Mister...." And before I could get the rest of it out, I was interrupted by "WHAT'S YOUR NAME LITTLE BOY?" He did not even let me finish or get it out. He snapped it at me with venom and poison, and I knew that this was no ordinary call. "WHAT'S YOUR NAME LITTLE BOY? You hear me?" I knew the answer, I promise you that I did, but the words got swallowed and re-swallowed. I hung up the phone and slammed it to make sure this was over. My grandmother heard the call and came running. "What happened?" I explained my failure to address this man properly and she shushed me. You know that definitive shush that ends all speaking and sound.

What is your name little boy? I said that I never got to say it and she said the following:

Remember this if you are my grandson. "Say your name! Say your name! Your name has power little boy, and never let anyone call you anything but your name."

What is your name little boy?

I cried. I was trying to process what just happened and what was happening at that moment. I was being loved on in a moment of need. I still did not get it until she said the next thing.

"It's not what you're called but what you answer to that matters. No one has the right to call you anything but your name. That is why I have been telling you this. Be prepared. There are folks who are mean and want to hurt people because they themselves are in pain. Your name is important. It was one of the first gifts given to you in this world. This is important. When someone calls you by anything else, remind them of who you are. Say your name."

My grandmother had been planting this seed for a long time. It was time for it to bear fruit. I called back and opened with my name. "Mister, my name is Derrick Pearson, and I apologize for not telling you my name before. I was caught off guard and got scared. Your name is Mister......, and my name is Derrick. I would like to speak to your daughter if that is okay. He was quiet. His voice rumbled and he delivered the news that I wanted to talk to her, and he surrendered his phone to her, for me. His daughter was stunned, as she had forewarned me that her father might not be happy with me calling. We talked for about ten minutes of shirt soaking nervousness and agreed to talk at school tomorrow. I chalked it all up to being a white neighborhood thing.

My grandmother hugged me with one of those hugs that cured everything. Those close your eyes and cry hugs Those shake you while hugging you hugs. Those we are all right hugs. She explained that using names puts everyone on the same level. It forces people to consider the other as a person. She also said that allowing your name to be dismissed or directed was always wrong.

She went on by saying that my name is how love is shared. She took a name out of love. She gave her children their names and shared those names with love and pride in full. She called those names to identify, and to elevate. She then flipped my brain by saying, "Your name is not who you are but where you come from. You come from me and your grandfather. You come from your mom and father. Your children will come from you. It means that you belong, you are worthy, and you are loved." More tears. More hugs. More love.

What is your name little boy?

I heard this before as a teenager. Moms and dads in the neighborhood. They used it out of curiosity. It was often followed by, "You can't date my daughter because you might be related!"

What? No one told me. I dismissed it as a Black neighborhood thing and left it alone. As I found out later in life, there was good reason for that question to be asked. My name is the same, but my origins are newly discovered.

My name is Derrick Pearson. My biological father's name is Garner. I am proud of both names. I am a Keaton. A Harris. A Green. And more. I am learning more about my name as I grow older, wiser, and smarter. I found out that my mother's real name is QUEEN ELIZABETH. I found out that had more siblings, cousins, and family. I found out that I was more loved than I knew or thought possible. I am the son of a Queen. I am the grandson of Hattie Sue Keaton Harris and Melvin Harris, Sr. I am the little boy raised by Roland Thomas Morgan, and his name is in my heart forever. I am the father of Aniko, grandfather to Nate, and husband to Rebecca.

Because of my grandmother, her love, and this journey, my family will know their names. They will also know where they are from, and who got them to where they are today. Everyone behind me will know my grandmothers name, her love, and story. This tiny legend loved entire blocks, entire families, and entire lives. She gave me a love for gospel music, an appreciation of the church, respect for the elders in her circle, and of myself. She gave me the power to be me, authentically. When I was choosing my college, she did not want me to go south. She was afraid. She said she would support me no matter what but make it clear that she was simply concerned that people would not care what my name was.

I went on a college recruiting visit to UNC-Greensboro in 1979. I was going to stop in Richmond on the way back and got my greyhound bus tickets for the trip. WHATS YOUR NAME LITTLE BOY? Sir, I am not little or a boy. My name is… I never finished. There was a Klan and Communist Party march/riot/massacre happening on the street. I took cover and waited. An hour or so later, I told the coach no thanks and started walking to the bus station to head home.

I made the next bus and sunk into my seat for the ride. Stop by stop, city by city, I counted the stops before Richmond. These were the days before cell phones, so I waited for a phone to become available. Yes. Good ole phone booths. I had forgotten one thing and never knew another. I forgot to call home to let them know that I was okay and heading north. I also did not know that the massacre was national news. They were worried sick. As I stood at the bus front door, those words landed again. What is your name little boy. I answered expecting more chaos. He instead reached his hand out and said, "Your mother is worried sick about you. She called every station to see if you had made a bus."

Every day in my profession, I get to say my name. I get to tell stories of who I am, where I am from, and who lived before me, for me, to better me. Every day, I think of this beautiful woman and her words. I think of her incredible heart and everlasting love. I love her for loving me and teaching me, because it is how I know that love can and should do that. Love is teaching. Love is caring. Love is a tiny goddess of a woman with the heart of gold and the backbone of a giant.

Here is to your Hattie Sue Keaton Harris. Here is to the lessons they taught, the love they gave, and the seeds planted in you that they were never able to see the fruit. Here is to your Hattie Sue. Her meals, her labors of love, her leading and guiding you to your best version. Here is to your great person. Here is to a life worthy of their love and their name. Your name.

What is your name little boy?

Hi. My name is Derrick Pearson. I am the son of a queen, and the grandson of AN ABSOLUTE GODDESS! Her name is Hattie Sue Keaton Harris.

What is your name?

ABOUT THE AUTHOR:

Social Media:
IG @derrickpearson
FB @derrick.pearson.5
Email pearsonderrick@aol.com

Derrick Pearson- Sports Radio Station Owner KNTK-FM Lincoln, Nebraska. Co-Host "Old School with Jay Foreman" "DP One on One" at 93.7 The Ticket FM Lincoln, Nebraska. Speaker-TEDxLander May 2019. The love Project Speaker-TEDxDeerPark March 2020. An American Face 3X Amazon Best Selling Author "The Impact of Influence, (Volumes 1&2) Rebuilt Through Recovery

Derrick "DP" Pearson brings his unique brand of energy to The Ticket's programming and direction. DP has spent stops during his career as a sportscaster, radio and television host, writer, manager, and high school coach. That career has taken him nationwide, including Washington, DC, Charlotte, Los Angeles, Salt Lake City, and Atlanta. In addition to his media and coaching ventures, he also helped establish Fat Guy Charities in Charlotte, an NFL Charity, and developed LovePrints, a national mentor program that promotes Loving and Learning through Sports. DP joins Jay Foreman every weekday from 8:00 am – 10:00 am. One on One with DP airs weekdays from 10:00 – 11:00 each weekday morning.

THE INFLUENCER
Jennifer Perez Solar

Influence
verb
influenced; influencing
transitive verb
1: to affect or alter by indirect or intangible means
2: to have an effect on the condition or development of

    Let's dive into the concept a bit further with the "influencer" that has reshaped our global community in unimaginable ways! The "influencer" being referred to here began in the first quarter of 2020. Some like to call it the year of vision. I like to call it the year of clarity! When we truly began to take stock in our lives, our career, and family. The period was coined as the Pandemic during this time of "influencer". For the sake of this chapter going forward, we will refer to the pandemic as the "Influencer".

    Each continent suffered losses and was affected equally, so the Influencer was also considered the great equalizer. Many decided to make this about politics though others decided to form support and prayer groups. We all had one common bond during the impact of this Influencer, Fear! One might say that as you dig deeper into your emotions, you will find fear. So, is this Influencer truly surviving based on fear?

A couple of years have passed since we have been introduced to the Influencer. Much has changed all over the world from how we travel to how we work. We have in most cases become more sensitive to our own personal lives as a result of being alone for a good amount of time. How have you done since? Where did you land after the Influencer changed us all? Is there more fear in your life or is there more curiosity, trust, courage, or acceptance?

When fear takes a hold of us, we begin to question the outcome of our future. If we learn to accept and move towards embracing this feeling of fear, then we can also learn to lean into acceptance and truly dissolve fear.

My personal story with the Influencer began a few weeks after my daughter's wedding and at the beginning of Quarantine for all of us. I woke in the middle of the night feeling very ill and gasping for air. This cough had been with me since the latter part of September 2019. We had no idea what the Influencer had in store for us at that time. I have a practice of writing and connecting with the Divine when I crave an extra boost of love and light in my soul. On this day, March 28, 2020, 4:45 am (I woke at 3:50 feeling very ill) as I sat in front of my computer, closed my eyes, and began to channel these words. As my fingers flew across the keys, it was as if the connection with my angels were all I needed to transcribe what I was hearing in my head. I become only the conduit for the divine connection. I wrote the following in my journal:

"I am strong and healthy. If the virus tries to enter, he will be in the wrong place. I am a fortress of my own body. Any illness that penetrates my loving walls will be sent love and then pushed along its way. There is no time for this for me. I am on the brink of discovery of who I truly am. I am a big part of this watershed. I will be here for the world and the humans on this planet. It is needed. I am the instrument of love and peace that this earth is looking for. Mother Earth is connected to me in a very strong way. What she feels, I feel. Please lessen the feelings so that I may rest now. Any and all negative forces that may be trying to wake me up should leave me now and let me rest so that I may continue my work tomorrow.

I am entering my universal quantum field Pin code. I am taking my place on the grid for this writing so that I may reveal the divine messages here now."

I continued writing the response that was returned:

"We are here for you. You are a queen of love and there is no match for your power on this earth. When you arrive to sit by us it will be only when your work is completed here. This is just the tip of the iceberg for you. You will create part of the new order. It will fall right into your lap, and you will be very instrumental in ensuring the children are prepared to arrive in our heavenly place. This is your true home and there is nothing to fear."

"Your entire family here on earth will also follow you here when their time comes. Your daughters chose you because it is their birthright. All your daughters. The humming in your left ear right now is reassurance that you are plugged into the grid now. This activation will protect you from this scare that your government is putting out there. It is serious and some people will die who are or are not ready. They will be walking through the beautiful heavens with angels as their guides. Everything there is perfect. The world that they could not be a part of here on this physical plain will be completely different and they are truly ready for this. Rest assured it is not for you yet. Your purpose here is to prepare the children so that they will enter the kingdom with genuine love in their hearts."

"Tomorrow, practice your energy routines, use your Colorlight tools on yourself, and build a pool for your joy. You do need the water now. Enjoy your time with your mother. Remember, you chose her to be by your side to witness your journey and she has. She is so proud. This is what you have to teach, the bond between mother and daughter. The bond between women and friends. This is why your daughters chose you, to teach you the bond of love between women."

"Love is love and it is pure. It is the strength that we have that helps us to carry on here on this human plain. This is why you have connected with so many women to discuss love on social platforms. Maternal love is the only true example of unconditional love. Mother Mary watches over you and your choices, which are to surround the children and other women with love. YOU were meant to lead them in the exercise of love and help each of them fulfill their passions here on earth so that they are prepared for their roles as guides when they transition to their new "soul home" places of love. Every day and in every way, you are being positioned to reach every one of them for a reason. When you wake each morning ask your guide Mother Teresa, 'Who is it that I am supposed to talk to today?'"

"It is no accident you see her name every day when you go to school as an elementary teacher. This is your constant reminder that you are a teacher, better yet, a guide to many! Go and rest now. See what tomorrow brings! You will be fine with very little sleep tonight. You are healthy and loving and full of grace. Amen dear child."

I shut my computer off and went back to bed. I slept well and deeply. When I woke up in the morning, I had a feeling of being refreshed! New and renewed. Even though the next year would be very challenging for us all I had confidence, and my heart felt reassured that I was here for a reason. It was more than a purpose. It was more like a passion for life.

A friend and I had been kicking around the idea of creating a small group of people to explore ourselves on a deeper level and taking action towards the things we dream of doing every day. We decided to meet on a virtual platform called "Zoom", which is where we met in a Mastermind, once a week. This was a large group of like-minded individuals who were craving change in their lives. Little did we know Zoom would soon be a way of life for us all. It was the Influencer that was causing people to become more isolated and quarantined from their jobs, families, and friends.

The more the Influencer spread its fear, the more we were isolated from in person interactions. Everyone scrambled to learn how to order food and household supplies, especially bulk orders of toilet paper, to take care of their needs. In some places, the grocery stores were closed to the public and only provided delivery. Many stores struggled to stay in business.

Amazon became a household name. Restaurants began offering incentives and coupons for delivery options. We were learning how to survive with very little movement. The internet and our cell phones became our lifeline to the outside world. Corporations scrambled to get their employees connected through virtual platforms and soon Zoom was a household name. Children were receiving all their education online in their own homes. We began to lose the human touch because we were in fear of being within 6 feet of each other.

Families were in their homes working and learning. This was both a godsend and a curse. We grew closer to our families, really began to think about how we were living our lives, and what we would like to do differently. The Influencer was in full force showing us all to become more than the fear and to understand the underlying messages of humanity. Soon, the Influencer began to take shape in new ways. People worried about getting ill. Many of us turned the worry into ways we could support each other by forming virtual groups to keep in touch and express our feelings.

My partner and I began a series of virtual classes to encourage people to reflect on their dreams and "refresh" them with new vision and hope. The classes were called Refresh Vision 2020. It was our way of guiding people to hit the refresh button on life and see things through their own imagination with a new viewpoint. To consider life in a new way with a new vision for the future. The more we created classes, the more we realized our purpose. Those who participated began to make changes to better their lives.

The Influencer gave us new insight. We became crystal clear on what we wanted our future lives to look and feel like. It seemed that as we faced fear of losing our health, we understood new ways to become healthier. The Influencer started a wave of good health and many alternative holistic health careers to emerge. As more people became sick, the majority became more health conscious and in turn healthier. Many lost loved ones, jobs, and homes through the hardships of the Influencer's broad reach.

There was so much trauma and toxic energy that more people turned to the simple ways of life such as farming their own foods, sewing, and creating works of art. Life began to be simple and pure once again. The animals in nature began to come out of hiding and were spotted in neighborhoods where they had not been seen before. The air seemed crisper and fresh. Outdoor activities were becoming the norm and exercise felt invigorating once again. We all began to breathe deeper and longer with the Influencers presence. It felt as though there was a shift from the hustling daily grind to a more relaxed way of life. Travel changed and people started to take long road trips to places in nature where they could hike, swim, and breathe again more deeply.

The Influencer has shaken us to our core and reminded us of our soul's purpose. Our passion for life has returned. We have since learned to take things slower and appreciate the moments together. While we still reflect on the Fear that crippled the globe for more than two years, we also know our authentic selves much better. We have walked through fear and embraced all that can be our future!

ABOUT THE AUTHOR:

Social Media:
IG @jennsolar1
Email Jenniferlsolar@gmail.com
Website www.allowandflow.com

Jennifer Perez Solar is referred to by friends and families as the local "sleep nanny"! Her career accomplishments range from healthcare corporate marketing to founder of a charter elementary school in the Tampa Bay Area.

She has over twenty-five years of experience in early childhood education and certifications specializing in newborn care. She has become an expert in mentoring young parents just starting their families, helping them raise healthy and loving children. Her own adult children have given back to the community in the areas of volunteering, childcare, and coaching in the sports arena. Watching her children follow in her footsteps, living happy well balanced adult lives, has made her realize that her ability to successfully raise children with love is her most valuable skill and profound purpose.

While the last fifteen years have been filled with caring for infants and young children, it became even more clear that her ability to soothe and settle babies and toddlers into a peaceful slumber is a trait that most young parents struggle with in their homes. Suddenly, she was being called a "sleep nanny". She is often contacted by young parents, near and far, to consult in the areas of sleep, conscious parenting, and ways to redirect behavior. Jennifer has also studied Samassati Colorlight Therapy. As a certified practitioner of Samassati and mindful intuitive, she has been able to share the use of color frequencies with light in a healing modality that truly activates the body's cellular health and an individual's emotional well-being.

Jennifer's soul's purpose is to transfer and enhance feelings of love and peace through mindful teachings to parents while building a strong foundation for the start of their lives together as a family!

TURNING NEGATIVES INTO IMPACTFUL POSITIVES
Jessica Perez

Have you ever been sized up or down? Have you ever been called insubordinate? Have you ever been told you weren't the right fit? Well, I have, and I am so grateful for all three of these experiences. These moments of loss created the shifts in the new roads and paths that I took. Let me share a bit about them as they have shaped me, refined me, and provided me with a different lens to view the world around. This inspired me to impact and influence others who may have experienced one, or all three of these challenging situations.

As a little fourth grader who loved sports, the boys who lived across the street used to let me play because I was fast, fearless, and super competitive on the court. I was accepted in their group because I was as skilled as they were. My younger sister was more into dolls than sports. One day she was crossing the street with her baby doll stroller when the neighborhood boys decided to pick on her and make fun of her. They were bigger than we were. They pushed her stroller over in the dirt and threw her dolls far away. They made a choice, sized me up, and figured I wouldn't do anything. Although I was an athlete, I was physically the smallest one of the group. They didn't realize that their actions would trigger a different response then what they had planned.

My sister didn't run away crying. She simply looked at me for support. That was it. A look from her signaling she needed help was the catalyst for a shift to occur. Me. The smallest one of the bunch, who had literally been sized down by this group of young boys. They thought that I would run away crying because I was a girl and smaller than all of them.

A line was drawn in the sand that day. There would be no turning back for me or my sister who watched me stand up for what was right and just. This 4'5" powerhouse rose and grew that day. I walked up to the older sixth grader who was the leader of the group and stood my ground. I told him to stop. He laughed and began to rally the rest of the boys to laugh as well. I took another step towards him and told him again to stop.

His response was the typical, "Why don't you make me?"

I did. Much to their surprise, little Jessica Perez balled up her fist and punched him in the nose. Guess what happened next? All the boys gave me a high five because he was the bully that no one had stood up to. It was the first day that the entire group realized that it was alright to be different or like different things. WE began to have each other's back that day. No one bothered my sister anymore. The boys didn't make fun of the slow kids or the ones that couldn't hit a basket. I am not proud that I used violence, but in that moment, the path to having moral courage, a moral compass that will steer me to always stand up for what is right was born.

Insubordinate. I never dreamed that would be uttered in a sentence with my name associated with it. I was truly shocked. I have been a rule follower since I was a kid going to Catholic school. You know the one: straight A's, never in trouble, didn't stay out past curfew, didn't drink till I was twenty-one. When that word was used, followed by the discussion that my body language gave the impression to others that I wanted the head of school's job, my head spun. I couldn't comprehend how we got there.

We were a group of passionate, caring, and dedicated folks who collaborated to create a school that was incredible in its first two years. As the school grew and became more well known, my role grew from founder and board member to teacher, coach, and building coordinator. I was very familiar with wearing many hats since I had previously been a teacher, athletic director, and coach at a small private school. As more students enrolled, additional needs surfaced. My sister, myself, and others found ourselves pushed into the forefront. Perception is an interesting thing. Since my overachieving actions spoke the loudest, it created this cloud of perceived importance. Some leaders took as a sign that I wanted to steer the parents and other faculty into following my lead instead of the head of school. Therefore, I was blindsided when this concept was shared with me.

If you have ever been a part of something significant, something that truly is life changing, then this part of this chapter is for you. When you shine brightly, others may see that glow as you attempting to dim their light, for yours to shine over theirs. I was raised with my two sisters by two parents who encouraged us to always do our best: in school, in sports, in clubs, as sisters, friends and family members too. The three of us were very different but we each had our own bright lights to shine. I excelled in school and sports. My older sister shined in political causes and career paths. Our younger sister flourished in her creative art and building of solid relationships. Dimming our light wasn't even a consideration for us.

It was engrained in me to show up. Literally, SHOW UP, fully and completely in anything that was along the path. To dim my light and not shine brightly was as foreign to me as speaking another language. As the motivational speaker and author Lisa Nichols says, "I am not dimming my light. I'm just going to hand you some shades."

Through coaching others, I have embraced my "glow", and will continue empowering others to embrace theirs. I believe we all have a lighthouse within us that is there to shine a light for all to see. Sometimes it takes just a simple word, like insubordinate, to catapult us to shine even more brightly than we knew we could.

The right fit? This is one of the most subjective phrases in hiring and firing situations. Initially, I was excited and flattered that I was hand selected to be the executive director for a not-for-profit organization. Having been recruited for eighteen months to leave a stable job to take on a new opportunity, I just knew this was my path to truly making a difference. They wanted me. They sought me out, created a compensation package that made sense, and filled my head with all the good stuff.

Six months later, a different perspective was shared. One that meant I simply "wasn't the right fit." Time for me to move on. Wait? What did they say? Move on? Yes, it was that easy for them. Lists of things I did or didn't do were shared. Ultimately, it boiled down to that simple short phrase, "You aren't the right fit."

I couldn't wrap my head around that comment. Recruited for eighteen months and in six months, not the right fit. Hmmm. Didn't make sense then and doesn't make sense now. Without that defining moment though, who I am, and what I do today would look a lot different.

Three very interesting experiences one in childhood, one in my thirties, and one in my forties. All of them necessary and allowed me to pivot, shift, to change the direction I was headed. While so many folks on the outside, could look at these moments in time as negative, I have chosen a less popular thought process. One that has provided me growth and self-awareness, that I wouldn't have had without these events. Were they challenging? Yes, but only briefly. Did they hurt my heart and self-worth? Yes, but only briefly. How many times have you allowed a circumstance, an event, or a situation to stop you in your tracks? To keep you and your mindset on a negative trajectory that doesn't align with your journey. It keeps you down and out.

I ask these questions so that you, like I do, will take a new approach when faced with negative experiences. The approach: create impactful positive ones instead of letting the negatives hold you back. For example, flipping the switch in our mindsets to expect challenges along the way. Staying grounded, living in gratitude, and nurturing the positive influencer within are ways to drive us towards a more meaningful, authentic relationship with ourselves and each other. There is nothing more rewarding than looking in the mirror and seeing that thriver smile back at you. Trust me. When you can own the negative, embrace all it did…that is where true impact and influence lives. Go ahead. I challenge you to take one, just one, of the negatives you have experienced and look through a cleansing lens. It will absolutely be the most freeing, enlightening, and enriching moment.

When you do, share that message with your circle. Let them know, you are on the path to true happiness. This my friends, is how life becomes even more inspirational as those negatives turn into impactful positives.

ABOUT THE AUTHOR:

Social Media:
IG @jessica_jlo_perez
FB @JessicaJLoPerez
Email perezjess141@gmail.com

Jessica Perez is a fourth-generation native to Tampa, FL who still lives, serves, and influences there. She grew up in a family-centered community that instilled the values of connection, relationships, loyalty, and impact. Jessica is a product of that "you can do anything" mindset, and she began a leaping journey to take on massive challenges in academics and athletics while growing through them.

Jessica graduated from St. Thomas University as a two-sport collegiate athlete and began her career in education as a physical educator, athletic director, and coach in private, public, and charter schools for eleven years. She co-founded Trinity School for Children in Tampa. She also dove into the non-profit world as a co-founder of CANDO Sports, Inc. over twenty-five years ago and still serves on their board. From education to local government, Jessica began a career with the City of Tampa as a Parks and Recreation professional. Her tenure included serving as manager for over two hundred employees, overseeing parks, a marina, community centers, pools, and art studios.

After a great career in both education and parks and recreation, Jessica dove into the world of entrepreneurism and network marketing. She has become a leader in her publicly traded wellness company named LifeVantage (LFVN) and is actively pursuing to speak, educate, and lead the charge in pioneering nutrigenomics while growing a leveraged global business. In addition, she is a certified trainer with the Positive Coaching Alliance and has delivered over four hundred workshops on the topics of leadership, coaching, and character development. She is much sought after as a coach, consultant, and catalyst for change.

LESSONS FROM THE COTTON FIELDS!
Johnny Martinez-Carroll

"Believe that it's possible"
-Les Brown

I grew up on a former cotton plantation in rural central Texas, in conditions that some would call humble beginnings. We had no running water or indoor plumbing. Thinking back to my childhood, we had very few things as far as material items are concerned. I had parents who believed in me. My dad talked me into getting in the electrical field and I have been an electrician for almost forty years now. I often wonder what career path I would have chosen had he not talked me into the world of electricity. Growing up in poverty certainly left me thinking that my options in life were limited. Poverty has a way of robbing you from the life you feel worthy of. I grew up in the cotton fields in the hot Texas summer heat. My dad never liked me working in the fields. He was the typical dad, wanting a better life for his son than he had experienced for himself. There's not a day that goes by that I don't remember that wood frame house and those cotton fields. Both of my parents influenced me to do my best and make the best of every situation. My dad once told me, "If you learn a trade, you will always have a job, and always have work."

He was correct. Dad was almost always on point with his advice, even though he only had a third-grade education. I grew up in some very humbling conditions. I am grateful for everything that I have been blessed with. My life has been filled with times of joy and times of hardship. Life in the cotton fields taught me to always be content. Growing up on a cotton plantation in poverty taught me to never take anything for granted.

A few years ago, I had my first book published, The Silent Dreamer. I wrote about transforming my life, from a high school drop out to a college graduate. My life has been filled with people who have influenced me by believing in me more than I ever believed in myself. People who reminded me that, "You do whatever you set out to do, you have what it takes!"

How does a high school kid go from dropping out to getting a college degree? If this had been left up to me, it would have never happened. I was working at a mental health facility in 1992 and enrolled in some GED classes. This was the year that I met a retired schoolteacher, Dorothy Crowson. Remember when I said my life has been filled with people who have influenced me? Ms. Crowson is one of those people. She taught me GED classes that year. I am not even sure if she is still alive today. I recall signing up for classes with her, along with 15 or 20 other students.

The class met with Ms. Crowson each week, on Mondays. Each week the class got smaller and smaller as students dropped out. Eventually there was one last man standing. Me. My life at that point had been filled with things I started but never completed. Would this be another to add to my growing list? Growing up I never really had a lot of confidence. I had spent years in the electrical field, only to get laid off from that job. I had mastered being an electrician over 8 prior to meeting Ms. Crowson in 1992. This sweet lady believed in me enough to come and teach this one student. She made me believe in myself.

It is an amazing thing when you believe in yourself. Ms. Crowson not only prepared me for the GED examination, just like the cotton fields that I grew up in, she prepared me for life. That life lesson is to never give up, the best will always come later! I remember taking the GED exam and passing it. I was so excited to finally achieve this accomplishment in life. The last conversation that I had with Ms. Crowson, she told me that I had what it takes, and she could see me enrolling in college courses. I never gave this a thought back in 1992. Again, when others believe in you it's a beautiful thing!

Fast forward twenty something years later, I enrolled in online college courses with The University of Phoenix. It took me a while to take the advice of Ms. Crowson. I was finally a college student. This sweet and wonderful lady would leave a lasting impact on me for years to come. This lady knew nothing about my past, she knew nothing about where I grew up, or how we lived in that house with no indoor plumbing. She knew nothing about how I always had intentions to go back to school and get that high school diploma. All she knew was that this young man had determination to get his GED, no matter how long it had been since high school. All that I knew was this retired schoolteacher believed in me!

A total stranger believed in me and thought that I could do anything that I put my mind to. Many years later, I still share my story of not giving up regardless of the circumstances around you. That same little boy who came from the cotton fields, believes in himself today. He believes that so much greatness lives on the inside of him, and that same greatness lives in others.

My dad believed in me as well. He demanded that I leave my job as a dish washer on Texas A&M campus and pursue a career as an electrician. I was speaking to a class of middle school students about a year ago. During a break between classes, a student walked up to me and asked if he could talk to me for a few minutes. I told him of course we could talk.

He asked me what my thoughts were on escaping poverty? How could a kid his age remove himself from poverty? I thought for a minute, then shared my story with him. I told him that education, in my opinion, was the key to defeating poverty. Even though school and education were not a big deal when I was growing up, I could clearly see the importance of it in my adult years.

The hot cotton fields could not break me. As a kid I would dream of a better life, a life that would put me in a good place, a happy place. Poverty can suck the life right out of you! It can take so much out of you. My current job as a case manager for a local non-profit, puts me in contact with hurting families, families that are either already in poverty or heading that way soon. Let me tell you that poverty does not discriminate. Most people that I know personally are one paycheck away from being homeless! It would not take much for them to hit hard times. Growing up in poverty I can relate to being in that situation.

The long cotton fields taught me that life is not fair. For the most part, we do not often choose the cards we are dealt with in life. As a young child, I would lay in bed at night looking out my window, wondering how this kid would leave the farm. What would life have to offer me outside the farm? As you are reading this, you may have wondered the same question, what does life have to offer you? Who is in your current circle of influence? What have you been putting off doing? Have you checked off your list of things that you have looked over for weeks, months, or maybe years now?

My father would say to me, "Always have an answer. Have a plan for everything."

I have often wondered, how did my dad, with a third-grade education, have so much knowledge to be able to teach and influence my life so much? I truly miss him. I miss that the people who believed in me as a child are no longer here to cheer me on and to see the accomplishments I have made in my life. Both my mom and dad would be so proud of their only son, the little shy kid who was literally afraid of his own shadow!

In my circle of influence, my parents sit at the top of the list. Everything that I do is to please them and so they would be so proud of me today. I drive by those same cotton fields every day on my commute to and from work. I glance over and say to myself, "I have so many footprints in those fields."

The same can be said about the people we meet daily. We have so many footprints that we leave in their lives, the people who we create friendships with, and share connections with. I walk away learning from everyone I encounter. Whether it's a friend or a co-worker, I learn from them and I hope they learn from me as well. I have been a published author since 2020. That's only two short years, but the wisdom and knowledge that I learned from authors who have more experience than me is priceless! That's how influence works, a never ending and always learning process.

I can honestly say that cotton fields taught me resilience and gave me a strong work ethic. I recall that for a couple of years I was a jobless, young dad, who was married with two small children. I had been laid off from work due to the economy, building was low, and the company that I was working for doing electrical work had a layoff. I was let go and had to make ends meet the best way possible. I started my own small electrical repair services, with no money or credit, but I had a lot of heart and talent.

Friends, this is the biggest lesson I learned in life, it does not take much money to do something, but it does take heart and desire to accomplish anything in life. I am a true believer that everyone is talented and gifted. We were all made for greatness and your gift will make room for you. The lesson about cotton fields is this, they are long and at times it feels like there is no end when you walk that row. Life can be the same, trials and tribulations come, and it appears there is no end in sight, but joy does come in the morning.

"Believe you can and you're halfway there"
-Theodore Roosevelt

Mindset is everything! I remind myself and I share this with others as well. Whatever we give time and energy to, becomes present in our lives. If you think and believe you will always be poor… guess what? You probably will always be poor. If you think sickness and illness all the time, you are probably not going to get well anytime soon.

    I have not always had this type of mindset; my thinking has not always been so positive. To be honest I grew up the very opposite. Poverty will affect you that way. Poverty will have you believing that you will never do better than your current situation. Believing in your self is a beautiful thing, it's so vital to your success in life. It's the one thing that can take you as far as you wish to go. The sky is truly the limit. I am so thankful for my circle of influencers, my parents whom I honor and write about in my books, my GED teacher, Ms. Crowson, who never stopped believing in me. I'm also thankful for my family, my wife, children, and grandchildren who continue to pour into me daily with never ending love. I would not be where I am at today without this support in my life, my friends who are close in my circle, who encourage me with love and support.

    There is never a day that goes by that I do not think of my deceased parents. I know they would have been proud of me. I know I mentioned this before, but I truly believe they would have loved how my life turned out. I never gave up, never made excuses for anything. I kept on going. There were many times I wanted to give in and quit. Maybe you have felt this way before as well, but never give up!

    As I close, I leave you with this, keep watering your dreams! Feed them and feed them often. You can achieve anything you want to in life if you only believe in yourself and continue the course. Stay on track. Your circumstances do not have control over your future. Remember, I came from the cotton fields. What matters is where you want to go in life. Where do you desire to end this destination in life? Remember, mountain top experiences begin in the valley! Never forget, you were made for greatness!

ABOUT THE AUTHOR:

Social Media:
IG @johnnymartinezcarroll
Email jmart777@msn.com

Johnny Martinez-Carroll lives in rural Central, Texas, in the small community of Snook, Texas. Johnny works for a non-profit, Methodist Children's Home out of the Bryan-College Station Outreach Office, where he works as a case manager.

Johnny Martinez-Carroll has published two books. His first book, The Silent Dreamer was released in July of 2020. His second, Pathway to Greatness, was released in August of 2022. Johnny shares his story of perseverance with young people and others who have struggled with life-changing obstacles. He went from being a high school drop out to a college graduate.

Martinez-Carroll shares his story of believing in yourself and surrounding yourself with people who encourage and empower you. He is a 2016 graduate from the University of Phoenix with a bachelor's degree in human services management. Johnny Martinez-Carroll is a certified life coach and motivational speaker. He facilitates a men's support group called Iron Sharpens Iron.

Johnny Martinez-Carroll enjoys giving back to the community by volunteering with local groups such as Habitat for Humanity, working with the homeless population in the Bryan College Station area, and providing food with Community Potluck. Martinez-Carroll is a husband, father, and grandfather. Johnny and his wife Sue enjoy family time with the grandkids.

DAMAGED GOODS: FINDING BEAUTY IN THE JOURNEY
Jordon Lewis

I can vividly remember, I couldn't stand up, I couldn't sit down, I couldn't lay down. The pain was excruciating. At five years old, I'd never felt anything like this in my few years of living. My parents tried everything, but I could not be consoled or made comfortable. My dad drove us to the emergency room at the local hospital and they admitted me immediately. The initial thought was appendicitis. After a CT scan, they found that I had torsion of my left ovary along with a mass the size of a grapefruit. The doctor advised that I needed emergency surgery to stop any opportunity of becoming septic and to reduce the chance of any advanced necrotizing infection.

At five years old my parents had to explain to me that I would have to be cut open to remove tumors, an ovary, and ultimately my appendix as well. The surgery was performed that same night. This was well before laparoscopic surgeries had been mastered. My incision was a low transverse, cesarean incision. Not the cute ones they do now, the almost hip to hip version. The tumor weighed a whopping fifty pounds. Prior to this surgery, my parents were convinced that I hadn't lost my "baby fat", but the culprit was much more serious. I remained in the hospital for four days. During my follow up visit with the doctor, they advised that tumors were benign, and this was something they had not seen before in a child my age. After a few weeks of recuperating, I was able to return to school and carry-on with life as normal.

My life became more unconventional as time progressed. My parents got a divorce a few years later and my life changed drastically. I could no longer attend the private school I'd attended since I was a few weeks old. We moved out of my childhood home, and to a few other locations around the Central Arkansas area. My transition during my teen years could be described as different. Due to having the oophorectomy, I began seeing a Gynecologist well before my peers. It was important to remain vigilant on my reproductive system since I was already at a disadvantage by having only one ovary. My hormones had to be checked and I had to have multiple ultrasounds to ensure no tumor activity was detected. My body progressed as a normal teenage girl and my Gynecologist decided that I was in the clear. He stopped the additional testing after turning fourteen, which ended up being a terrible mistake.

I turned sixteen and the decision was made that I would move to my dad's home. After moving in with them, I began having pains in my lower abdomen, which alarmed my dad, knowing my gynecological history. He took me to a different Gynecologist to determine why I was having the issues and four tumors were found. We had a follow up that same week. The doctor decided to do another ultrasound just to make sure. He found that the tumors had doubled in size. He advised that it would be necessary to remove my remaining ovary. At this point, the doctor began to discuss a new syndrome that was becoming more prevalent in the black community among young women called PolyCystic Ovarian Syndrome (PCOS). This was the first time I'd ever heard of PCOS, after being diagnosed with it.

My second surgery was performed the following Saturday and the recovery was much tougher than my first time. Due to my previous incision, the doctor used the classic incision style for this surgery. The scar went from my belly button down, cutting through my abdominal muscles. I was confined to a recliner to aid in the ease of getting up to go anywhere. I couldn't move without assistance. It took about six weeks for me to be able to return to school and an additional four weeks to resume normal activities. I also had to come to terms with the fact that I would remain on a low dose formulation of birth control to regulate my hormones. My life would never be the same, because medically I could not have children naturally. This was not a big deal to me as a teenager. As I got older, it was something I became ashamed of.

I'll pause at this point to answer questions that have been asked multiple times, after retelling my story. Neither of the gynecologists ever discussed harvesting my eggs before removing my ovaries. I'm not sure why, but this was never brought up. I am the only child of my mother and father. The ability to receive a donor egg from a sibling was possible, but the child and I would not share the same genetic make-up. My mother was also diagnosed with PCOS after me, but no other family members, that I know of, suffer with the syndrome. Now back to the story.

I can recall a church member disclosed the information regarding my surgery to others and made it seem as though I'd "done something" for this to be my plight. I was utterly embarrassed and did not care at the time to clear up the misconception. As I stated before, PCOS was not as well-known as it is today, so explaining my condition to others was a chore and many times I chose not to disclose it to others. It was my scarlet letter, something abnormal. Women had babies and that opportunity had been stolen from me at just sixteen. As I began to mature and enter relationships, I would end up having to discuss my "problem", for full disclosure. Many men had no issue with it, because in college, no one is looking or planning for marriage, right? I got more comfortable telling my story and it became less of a burden to do so.

While in college, I also made the decision to allow my body to naturally progress through menopause. I stopped taking the birth control pills because I didn't see the need for them. I can honestly say, everything women say about menopause is TRUE. To experience this as a college student was pure torture! Though miserable, I was at peace, because I felt this was a part of my journey. PCOS had robbed me of a chance at motherhood, or so I thought. I knew eventually I'd need to progress to a stronger hormone regimen, and I was not interested in that. I took things into my own hands, and I must say, I have no regrets about it, now.

At some point, I came to grips with the fact that I would not be able to have children the "natural way". It definitely took some time for me to fully settle in it and be ok with that truth - my truth. In 2010, I met the man that would eventually become my husband. At that time, he was not considering settling down, let alone having children. Our initial relationship was very short lived, maybe three months, so the conversation about my inability to reproduce never came up before we went our separate ways.

Life happened for both of us, and we reacquainted in 2017. By this time, he had a daughter but neither of us had been married. As we grew closer, I decided to have "the conversation" with him. I was apprehensive, because we were barely thirty, had matriculated through graduate school, and both intended to live an abundant life. In my mind, abundance meant having a family that included children. To my delight, he was not interested in having additional children, I mean he was resolute with his decision. Later, he would inform me that he wasn't sure if I was as firm about not having children. He wanted to make sure before we got too serious, because he was NOT having more children.

In marrying my husband, I received a gift that I never thought I'd experience. Being a bonus mom to an amazing child is an undertaking that is not for the weak. It certainly has its own set of challenges, but I would not trade it for the world. I can engage daily, challenge, rear, and guide a child, which unfortunately is a process that many take for granted. I do not. Let me be clear, under no circumstances have I ever attempted to replace her birth mother, but she knows, as well as everyone that knows us, that I love her just as if I bore her myself. In fact, I'd move mountains and go to war with anyone behind her! I literally learned that becoming a mother has nothing to do with carrying a child, it comes with caring for a child.

Although I did not think my life would ever look like it does today, I'm eternally grateful.

I'm grateful for the challenges. Having PCOS before it was a "thing", or a notable syndrome was difficult. The problems I faced only having one ovary, then having none, making the decision to allow my body to go through menopause at twenty-two, giving up the opportunity to have children "naturally". These decisions were hard, it was tough, but it has made me the woman I am proud to be today. Anytime I hear that someone close to me has been diagnosed, especially if I have not had the opportunity to share my story, I reach out and offer my support. I'm able to share from a place of walking in shame and emerging from the shadows of a syndrome that has taken so much from so many. I have lived this struggle, and everyone's story does not look like mine, but I proudly and boldly speak my truth. I will let anyone know that I've dealt with PCOS for over 30 years, but I did not allow it to write my story. In the beginning, I thought of it as a plague, my scarlet letter, but today I affirm that it did not steal anything, it enhanced my life and is a part of my beautiful journey.

ABOUT THE AUTHOR:

Social Media:
IG @jordonthegenie
Email jjlindustriesglobal@gmail.com

Jordon Lewis is a lifelong resident of Central Arkansas. She has worked in the Healthcare Industry in various capacities for over twelve years and in management roles for a majority of that time. She is currently an employeeprenuer with plans to officially retire from Corporate America by December 31, 2022. She is currently the Chair of L&J Empowerment, Inc. and The Lewis Family of Businesses.

Jordon holds a Bachelor's of Science in Health Professional Promotion from the University of Arkansas at Monticello and a Masters of Health Administration from South University in Savannah, GA.

Jordon married her best friend in April 2020 and enjoys spending time with her Husband, Lorenzo; bonus daughter, Sareya; and four-legged son, Maximillion. She is a lover of all things pink, sparkly, and a maker of pretty things! When not working, Jordon enjoys listening to audiobooks, crafting, being a Genie, spending time with her family, and traveling.

A DREAM BACKED BY HARD WORK
Jose Escobar

My parents Raul and Aracely Escobar immigrated to this country from Guatemala over forty years ago. They came here with no money, nowhere to live, basic education, and no understanding of the English language. The one thing they did bring with them was a dream. They had the American dream of raising a family in the USA. The success that this land of opportunity can provide was what they were after. They just wanted a shot to make something of themselves and provide a legacy for their kids and future generations.

My parents have now been happily married for over forty-eight years. I have three brothers, Christian, Michael, and Tony. I am first-generation here in the USA, born in Washington DC. Yes, I am a die-hard Washington Commanders fan. I grew up watching the Washington Redskins every Sunday on my dad's lap. My Dad was quite the sports enthusiast. He loves to follow any team representing our Nation's Capital. Truth be told, his true passion in the sports world is soccer.

My mother Aracely came to this country and her first job was cleaning houses. She would clean upwards of three to four fancy homes a day. Many times, she would take me and my younger brother with her if we didn't have a babysitter. I am pretty good at cleaning and consider myself to be an organized person, perhaps because of watching how my mother cleaned these homes so meticulously.

She would come home exhausted after a long day of housecleaning. Then had to care for four young boys at home in our small apartment. I shared one bedroom (bunkbeds) with my brothers for the first ten years or so growing up. We grew up as a family tight with money, but my parents always found a way to provide for us. We always had food on the table, clothes on our backs, and a roof over our head. Most importantly, my parents gave us all the love we could ever ask for and the foundation of our Catholic faith. They went above and beyond to show us how to live virtuous lives.

I can humbly say that I am the man I am today largely in part of how my parents raised me. I am a faithful husband to my beautiful wife Katie, and a devoted father to my 5 kids, Noah, Zelie, Avila, Siena, and Judah. Growing up I always saw how my Dad loved my Mom. Not just in words but in his actions. He was a great leader in our home. Never did drugs, didn't drink alcohol, never went out with "the boys", and was one heck of a hard worker and provider. My Dad worked like two to three jobs at a time for decades to provide for us all. When he first came to this country, he was building homes, then got into the restaurant industry. He started out as a dishwasher and moved his way up the ladder in just about all positions a restaurant would have to offer. Eventually over thirty years later he would own his first restaurant. My Dad always went above and beyond with anything he set his mind to.

My Mom would eventually start her very own business when I was around seven years old. She had a friend who was trying to recruit her into a business called Jafra Cosmetics. This is a multi-level marketing company (competitor to Mary Kay). For many years my Mom declined to join. She felt it was not for her. She would say things to herself like, "I am not a salesperson. I am shy. I don't have what it takes. It sounds too complicated." Until one day she got the itch to ask one of her mentor friends what her opinion was.

This friend happened to be someone who she worked for. My Mom would clean her house for years. She asked her what she thought about her starting this business. Shockingly, she was told, "don't start that business. Just stick to what you're good at. Cleaning houses is what you do and all you will ever do."

Wow! My Mom was appalled by this response and went home to tell my Dad about it later. She was so hurt by these words. This fueled the winner inside her that lay dormant. My Mom decided to start the business in the midst of doubt, fear, lack of skills, lack of resources, limited time, etc. My Dad would go on to support her as well on this new journey.

That was the beginning of a business empire my Mom would go on to build. A few years into building this business as a side hustle while still cleaning homes, she eventually grew it big enough to where it became the primary source of income for our family. It became a multi six-figure enterprise that would scale across the country from coast to coast. She won numerous awards, traveled the world, trained and spoke to thousands of leaders across the country, and became a powerhouse businesswoman. This was only possible because she had the courage to take action to get started and the perseverance to weather all storms along the way. Trust me, there were many trials and tribulations along the way, but that's the path an entrepreneur chooses for that next level in life.

My parents really built something special in this life. They bought their first single family home in Rockville, Maryland, a few years after the Jafra business was taking off. Eventually my parents went on to purchase a million-dollar home in Brookville, Maryland. I like to call it their dream home. We lived there as a family for many years. So many great memories were created there. Today, my parents are now retired and traveling. They achieved many goals and dreams while paving quite a path for my brothers and I. Words cannot express how grateful I am for their love, leadership, and commitment to our family. They have done so much for us all.

This reader's digest short version of my parents and our story as a family is being told because it has truly made a tremendous impact on my life. By default, it has now impacted many lives around me that I now influence. Watching my parents as I was growing up has inspired me in so many ways that are hard to articulate. They showed me what hard work means. They defined perseverance, grit, determination, tenacity, discipline, focus, consistency, commitment, and above all, love. They lived these words every day. Words are words, but they showed me through action as well. They have taught me so much in this life which is imprinted on my heart and I'm forever grateful.

Today I am implementing much of what I learned from my parents. I have taken all the good they showed me and created my own spin through tons of personal development and mentorship. I am the Founder and CEO of The Entrepreneur's Bookshelf and the Connected Leaders Academy. Both companies have surpassed six figures in under seven months and are scaling every day. I have a Morning and Evening Routine Mastery Program whereby I coach tons of people helping them improve their mindset, health, and productivity. It's an eight-week program and on the other end of the eight weeks my clients walk out with their very own customized morning and evening routine. It's changing lives and helping many improve both personally and professionally. I am also an international best-selling author and have co-authored five books. I also have my own book I wrote, "Winning The Day: An Entrepreneur's Guide to Morning & Evening Routine Mastery."

The Connected Leaders Academy is a subscription-based membership I launched for entrepreneurs. I have scaled it to over 220 members in 11 countries and 34 states coast to coast across the United States (as of this writing). It is composed of high-level entrepreneurs who joined for five reasons; to grow both personally and professionally, scale their influence, move the needle in their business (more clients/more money), develop their skill sets and expand their network. The CLA is a tribe of high-performers, influencers, titans of industry and successful leaders. I am now in the events space as well. I have the first ever CLA Global Summit coming up in October 2023. We will have 1000+ entrepreneurs in attendance from around the world.

I launched a merchandise line of branded products supporting both my companies as well. Things like t-shirts, sweatshirts, bookmarks, coffee mugs, journals, etc. I have a one-on-one coaching business as well. Just recently got Maxwell certified as a coach, trainer, and speaker. I am also doing about two to four speaking gigs a month these days and putting on Pop Up live events. All these moving parts have allowed me to really grow as an entrepreneur. All of what is happening now I owe to the influence my parents had on me growing up. Watching them look at the end of their own arm for help and rolling up their sleeves to get the job done with zero excuses. I went from having an average job with just about "average" everything to scaling my companies to over half a million in a year and projections of seven figures by June 2023. I am beyond blessed and eternally grateful to God, my parents, my amazing wife, and all those whom I serve.

I have taken my parents' leadership and high-level influence to be the foundation from where I stand today. I am a servant leader and heart-centered in all I do. I am here to help others become their best and realize their dreams. Zig Ziglar said it best, "you can have everything in life you want if you will just help enough other people get what they want." It is just that simple. I am on a mission to create global impact and help as many people get to their next level as possible. This calling has been placed on my heart. I fully intend to rise to the occasion and fulfill God's calling for me. There is much work to be done. I believe in divine intervention and those whom I'm meant to serve will cross my path at some point or another.

If you are reading this and asking yourself how you can level up and get to that next stage of success, let me give you some quick tangible tips. Make up your mind with a full-blown commitment that you are going after it all. Identify what you want. Your dreams, goals and mission in life lies on the other end of discomfort and commitment. Don't just decide because you can decide the next day then change your mind. Fully commit to a new you and what you desire to achieve. Then create a life plan. What will your life look like going forward? In terms of the success habits you will install, and discipline that will be required. Write this plan down on paper and ask yourself the tough questions.

1. What do I need to give up to get what I want?
2. What will my morning and evening routine look like?
3. Who do I need to let go of in my life?
4. Where do I need to reinvest my money so it works for me?
5. How will I work on my health so I can perform at my best?
6. How will I improve my relationship with God?
7. Who do I need in my life that can mentor me?
8. What addictions or poor habits in my life need to be cut loose?
9. What is my growth plan for personal development?
10. How will I structure my spare/nonproductive time wisely?

These are just a few questions that can get you on the right track towards creating a plan that will work for you. Next, take massive action on your plan. Stop procrastinating and start getting used to making executive decisions quickly. Your time is now. Nobody will believe in you until you believe in you! Stop waiting for someone to cosign what belongs to you and go get yours. Trust me, people will start to follow once you choose to become worth following. John Maxwell says it best, "Leadership is influence." Decide what you want by setting some goals. Create a detailed plan by asking the tough questions and take massive action.

Your best life is one commitment away. I am so excited about where my life is today.

My Dad used to always tell me, "Take one day at a time."

My Mom used to always tell me, "Mistakes are paid in cash."

I have taken away so much from their example and wisdom. They've cemented many of their own quotes in my life through the years. I could probably write a book about it. My life is mission based these days. I've been abundantly impacted for the good through my parents' influence. It is with great pride and joy that I continue to carry the torch and influence others to be their best as we create great impact for the good in this world.

ABOUT THE AUTHOR:

Social Media:
IG @jaesco25
FB @jaesco25
Email jaesco25@gmail.com

Jose Escobar was born in Washington, DC and resides with his family in Maryland. He is happily married to his wife Katie Escobar. Together they have five children. Currently, he is the Sales Director for the Educational Funding Company (EFC). Jose is the Founder and CEO of The Entrepreneur's Bookshelf. His best-selling program, "The Morning & Evening Routine Mastery" has generated over six figures in only five months. He is also the Founder of The Connected Leaders Academy that has surpassed the six-figure mark in under seven months and is rapidly growing its members globally. Jose is a best-selling author, speaker, and high-performance coach.

OUR JOURNEY TO VICTORY
Joshua Ogunyemi

"You have a very sick baby."

"We've done all we can do."

"You should consider terminating care." That's what the neonatal specialists told us about our baby, Kennedy. Kennedy and her identical twin sister, Morgan, were born on January 21, 2013, after only twenty-three weeks of pregnancy. Morgan was born at 1 pound, 3.4 ounces; Kennedy was born at 1 pound, 3.7 ounces. Morgan passed away shortly after, just a day after birth; however, Kennedy continued to fight! The next six months were a mental, physical, spiritual, and emotional rollercoaster ride. It was riddled with ups, downs, highs, lows, the good, the bad and sometimes, the downright ugly. There were laughs, cries, hard days and harder days, uneventful days, and close-calls. My wife, Michelle, and I were finally able to bring our baby home from the neonatal intensive care unit (NICU) with no tubes or extensive equipment and our journey to victory began.

Keep smiling!

We are all familiar with the song, "If You're Happy and You Know It (Clap Your Hands)." It has become one of our household favorites. And my favorite part of the song is, "If you're happy and you know it, SMILE. If you're happy and you know it, SMILE. If you're happy and you know it, then your face will surely show it. If you're happy and you know it, SMILE!"

At face value, this "happy" song seems to contradict what appears to be a somber story. After addressing some sobering details, how can I, and why would I suggest 'keep smiling?' Well, I will tell you why we continue to smile. Throughout our entire experience, and to this day, we have found reasons to smile. We still have our faith and our hope! We're still standing, trusting, and believing in God's Word.

To be honest, I can think of so many times we had to rely on a smile, a laugh, and the joy of the Lord which has always been our strength. That strength that kept us going empowers us every day. It gives us the strength to bounce back and keep going. I thought it was important for you to know that no matter life's circumstances, we will keep smiling! Grammy Award winner, Kirk Franklin said it best in his song "I SMILE":

> *"I smile, even though I hurt, see I smile.*
> *I know God is working so I smile.*
> *Even though I've been here for a while,*
> *I smile. Smile!"*

It has become important that we remember to smile every day. And I encourage you to Smile like you mean it! You may have had a tough week. I know sometimes it's a struggle just trying to get a smile through. Whatever you do, just smile. Remember, you are strong enough to conquer whatever you are going through and come out better than before!

Do me a favor: look in a mirror, or take a selfie with your smartphone, and smile as wide as you can! Show yourself that beautiful smile. While you're still smiling, take a deep breath and make a concerted effort to focus on three positive things going on right now–even if that list begins with, "I am still breathing." Take a few minutes of slow, controlled breaths, and allow the brightness of your smile and your positive thoughts to permeate your mind. This is the attitude and mindset we will take along our journey to victory!

YOU were made for this!

We would learn that, because of her extreme prematurity and trauma at birth, Kennedy would require long-term care. This included physical and other therapies, drugs, and surgeries. She would experience AND overcome many more challenges throughout her life. Years later, doctors diagnosed her with Cerebral Palsy, a condition characterized by spasticity in her muscles, causing challenges with her movement and mobility. But from the beginning, our mission has always been for Kennedy to live a full and healthy life.

For me, it has been a pleasure "doing the hard work," working with her to overcome those challenges. Taking the time to appreciate, honor, love, cherish, and labor with our daughter has revealed patience and inner strength to overcome challenging situations. It has given me courage to face adversity and a formula for success through tough times. Being persistent when confronting challenges head on brings out the best in you! These moments reveal resilience that helps you transform situations that you previously could not transform. We are blessed to create impact and affect change in situations that seem out of our control.

It's through our many challenges that we develop character and sharpen our gifts. Challenging times tend to consume us when we don't view them in context. Yes, several doctors told us that Kennedy would be "severely deformed" and "handicapped." They told us all the "bad news". They told us that her chances for survival were extremely low, and to raise her (one doctor concluded) would be "a rollercoaster."

Those words can be terrifying and intimidating for two young first-time parents. Although we were at the beginning of our life together, I am most proud that we stood together and accepted our assignment. As I said in my book, *tough times don't last, TOUGH PEOPLE DO,*

*"Rollercoasters are fun! We have had **a blast** raising Kennedy. Yes, it's been scary at times. Yes, it's been a bumpy ride. But that's why we love rollercoasters, right?! We stand in line patiently for ' it doesn't matter how long,' **push past the fear and anxiety**, then buckle ourselves in and **enjoy the ride**. That's the mindset you have to take into your tough times."*

Our gifts were made for this moment!

Through our journey to victory I have learned to recognize and appreciate many of the innate gifts that we ALL share. Particularly, the ability to manifest –the power to heal, the power to create, bring things to life. Manifesting begins with what we think and speak. I have become careful and intentional with my words. I treat my words like seeds that will grow (manifest) into fruitful trees.

God blessed us by bringing Kennedy into our lives! She gives our family a clear sense of purpose and pride. We were chosen for the assignment. Likewise, YOU were hand-picked for your assignment. YOU are equipped for the mission. YOU are built for this, and God trusts YOU!

We learned that with Kennedy, God trusts us to be informed and make sound decisions regarding her health and safety. That gives us confidence in any situation. We know that God trusts us to make the right move and get the job done.

The doctor who witnessed it all.

I am so proud that a couple of years ago, we were able to visit one of the same doctors who previously told us in a deep gravelly voice, "She's a very sick baby." He saw her born at twenty-three weeks at one pound and three ounces. Kennedy survived the passing of her identical twin sister. She also suffered a Stage 4 hemorrhage–the worst form of bleeding from the brain. At that time, her body was too fragile to undergo the life-saving surgery that would keep her alive, so specialists used a needle to withdraw fluid from her brain to reduce the pressure and swelling.

The team of doctors had encouraged us to terminate care, but we remained hopeful. We chose to stand in faith and believe in God. When they admitted, "we've pretty much done all we can do… It's essentially our efforts keeping her alive [and] it's probably best if you let her go." My wife recalls that I responded, "Y'all do what y'all do, and we'll do what we do– pray and stand on God's Word." Since then, Kennedy has made science-defying strides–proving that faith works.

Faith in Action

It's our responsibility to heal the world around us.

Many of us are familiar with the biblical story about a rich ruler who divided up talents among his workers and left town for a while. When he came back, the two he gave multiple talents to gave him back more than what he had given them. But, there was one who gave him back the same talent that he had been given. The Master was displeased with the servant who did nothing to multiply his talent.

Why? Because God wants us to take our situations–the gift that He's given us–and give him back more!

God works through us!

I believe that the power of God heals, cures sickness and disease and sets the bound free, but it is by our hands that these miracles happen. It is by our hands that we manifest miracles, signs and wonders. Scripture says God is able to do exceedingly abundantly above all that we can ask or imagine according to the power that works IN US (Ephesians 3:20).

Remember the doctor I told you about?

Yep, one of the few who thought that turning down the assignment was even an option. We visited him seven years later. He was amazed at Kennedy's speech and cognition she displayed during the conversation. He had some questions! This doctor remembered her brain scans all too well. It looked like she didn't have a chance! He remembered the conversation we had too. You know, the one where he encouraged us to terminate care.

That same doctor said that based upon what he saw, Kennedy shouldn't be this far along. She shouldn't be doing the things that she's doing. As a matter of fact, he didn't think she would make it. At best, he expected her to be "severely retarded" and unable to walk or talk. He originally told us that she'd likely be a vegetable and would need a lifetime of drugs, machines, oxygen, and around-the-clock care.

Kennedy's [our] journey to victory!

Instead, after six months of being in the NICU, she came home with no equipment, oxygen, medicine. It was almost like she came home and said, "that was it??" Today, Kennedy is on the A/B Honor Roll, promoting grades with her age group, and can even count in Spanish! She sleeps comfortably in her own room–in her own bed–and she is a prayer warrior. Kennedy quotes scriptures and recites positive affirmations every day. She will also get you together, whether you ask for it or not.

The doctor told us that he believes Kennedy would not be where she is had she been in any other hands. I believe our journey to victory began when we realized our power to manifest and transform any situation!

The revolutionary perspective that can change the world!

This belief has revolutionized the way I approach life, my family, and even my professional career! As a creative, I get to bring ideas to life and I approach every project the same way: I assess the need, affirm my goal, and commit to learning something in the process. Then, I take action transforming the idea–believing in my ability no matter how challenging the project. It never gets old; taking a step back and looking on in amazement as the idea I spoke life into manifests.

Believe it or not, YOU have this same power! Walk confidently knowing that you can transform any situation.

YOU have the power to heal.
YOU have the power to create.
YOU have the power to bring things to life.
YOU have the power to make a positive difference in this world!

ABOUT THE AUTHOR:

Social Media:
IG @josh.ogunyemi
FB @joshua.d.ogunyemi
Email Joshua_ogunyemi@yahoo.com

"Josh O." is a devoted husband, dad, mentor and entrepreneur. He is proof that faith, courage, and determination will outlast even the toughest challenges. His story has inspired many, exemplifying spiritual and mental toughness, defying every challenge he's had to face.

Despite losing a child, periods of unemployment, failures, financial problems, the everyday pressures of marriage and fatherhood, and raising a child with special needs, he has become a champion of challenging situations and encourages others to do the same.

MY ISLAND
Dr. Lindsie O'Neill Almquist

It's a beautiful crisp Saturday morning. The chimes my Mom and Daddy Jimmy (DJ) bought us are making music in the breeze. It's October 2022, and our babies are enjoying the amazing weather as they color and play out on the patio. So far only one sibling tiff, so I will take it. Sometimes I pinch myself. This cannot be real. I did not deserve this. I soak it all in knowing it can all be gone in a second.

My babies are four and five. They are everything you can imagine and more. Ellis Blake is our eldest. She is our shooting star; born January 1st. Briggs Leon is our son. He was born eleven months later. Irish twins. Yes. They were born within the same calendar year, and it was crazy! It was also the most beautiful mess of a blessing. One of those things that you realize was the hardest and greatest thing in your life, all at once. You know those things.

My husband and I were thankful that this day wasn't full of to dos. It was my precious father-in-law's birthday. His first in Heaven. This week was the first anniversary of my sweet Papa passing and now we were faced with our Dad's first birthday gone. The past year had almost did us in. You know those years? The ones where you really can't believe it was the slowest dang year, yet it was the fastest? One thing is for certain though. It was devastatingly heart wrenching. We lost three precious dear souls all within three months and two just within nine days of each other. We got too good at writing obituaries and working with funeral homes, that's for sure.

My precious husband has been the most beautiful soul through it all. On his birthday last year, he held my Papa's hand as Papa was getting closer to going Home. The intent of a spouse is to be a partner, but Cody's life has become so much more than that for me. The impact of his life in mine has been the most steadfast and sacred model of influence. It's from Jesus Himself. I know that without a doubt.

One vivid example is during the many long months of waiting to be parents. We trekked the devastating mountains of infertility. For anyone struggling, I stop right now and pray. My heart longs for your blessings, pains for your hurting, and deeply and genuinely hopes for your miracle. Remember me saying Ellis was our shooting star? That's because she was a five-day blastocyst. She was made with a lot of love and some science. As an ICSI IVF baby, she went from having a petri dish as a home, to being shot into her little warm humble abode of my body. If none of this makes sense, just be grateful. On the monitor she was a shooting-star. It was the most surreal moment of our journey. She is a daily reminder that God fulfills His promises.

Four months after Ellis was born, on Good Friday 2017, we found out we were pregnant again. Shocked doesn't describe it. I remember the day like yesterday. Ellis and I had a day full. We got her ears pierced, then bought Easter eggs and candy for our Easter get-togethers. I had looked forward to the day I could take my baby girl to have her ears pierced and it was the day! It was an honor that one of my former students performed the piercing. I was so excited to see some of my life as a principal and mom come full circle. A few hours after our momentous ear piercing, we found out that another baby was on the way. I remember calling Cody. We were like ... what? How? Lovingly and supportively, he talked with me on the phone call. We went about our Easter activities seeing many family members and we remained quiet. If you know me, that was very difficult. I was so sick. I was a hot mess and there was not much "express" in me at the time. Eight weeks after Ellis was born, we conceived Briggs. Cody's love through that journey taught me what a true partnership is. He was, and still is the encouragement and faithful counterpart, where we are all in this together. I never felt alone. His influence of grace and compassion is something I am forever grateful for.

While I know our journey isn't everyone's, please know that YOU will have your promises fulfilled as did Abraham in Hebrews 6:15. It's tattooed on my left wrist. It changed me. Eternally. I grew in faith, hope, and love. Empathy in my life grew from that experience. In every moment of my day, I am thankful for the lesson of humility, and the positive difference we can ALL make with a little bit of grace and empathy.

Now, back to my tall glass of water. Cody is a unique being. He is a gentle giant. A calm in the storm. A quarterback. A solid (Easter) bunny. He is the softest, kindest soul that sticks to his core, and yet the strongest fighter when life gets tough. He was the Homecoming King in Hippo Nation (a precious school district Northeast of Austin, Texas). To be honest, NEVER someone I would have ever thought about in high school. He is so much more than anything I could have ever dreamed of. Life is a whirlwind. Cody is just who I needed.

God sure knew what He was doing by bringing Cody in my life. Before meeting him and after a very broken heart, I wasn't anywhere near my best. One July night I stopped, dropped, and pivoted. I had a heart to heart with God, and a heart to heart with myself. I knew (and still know) Rome wasn't built in a day, and neither would my trajectory change. Then, a few weekends after that, as I was helping my girlfriend move out of her duplex to start her teaching career, my life was changed forever. Cody also showed up to help her move. To be honest, it wasn't love at first sight. He was late and I had to wait. Not impressed.

What happened after that moment was a pure miracle. The impact of Cody's life on mine has been substantial from that moment. I have come to learn that true love does NOT cause pain. Instead, it heals, soothes, and loves through the hardest of times, and the easiest of days. It is a rare love. I am aware of that. I am completely humbled. Honestly, up until a few years ago, I still didn't think it could be true. I thought I would wake up one day, he'd be gone, and we'd be over. It can still happen. I know that. If that were to ever happen, I've been beyond blessed with the impact he has already had in my life. I don't need Cody. I want him, and vice versa. Big difference.

We have a lot of life to live, but one thing is for sure, Cody shows up, and he is the most influential person in my life. He has shown grace to people that many would turn their back on. He has honored people after they have done nothing but hurt his spirit and heart. Cody has clear boundaries and knows what he wants in life. He is a wonderful husband and father. He shows his love through his gentle, quiet spirit of a huge heart.

The day we found out that having babies may not be in the cards for us, a bit of me died inside. As I write these words, the heartache comes to my eyes as these teardrops fall. It crushes the strongest willed and hardest working souls. I wasn't having it. My years in high school and college were filled with foster siblings, predominantly brothers. I knew from those experiences that I wanted children. Any way I could. For us, we wanted to pray about it, and seek medical attention. The Kovoussi brothers in Austin, Texas, and their amazing team were absolute blessings. We traveled back and forth for weeks (and learned that P Terry's was our jam). Our sweet embryologist was Ellis' first babysitter in that tiny petri dish. What a job right?!

I remember watching my dear love hear the outcome of our medical diagnosis. Again, he showed up. He didn't falter. Gentle giant. Six foot four inches with hands that work in the extreme heat on disgusting machines. There he was, with the frailest, loving, kindest spirit. He stopped, dropped, and pivoted. He made those mountains feel like stepping-stones. Our daily reminder that, a positive mindset, a clear focus, and a lot of prayer will provide the direction and momentum to be in a different space. One day at a time. Infertility will kill you. Divorces exist because of it. Marriages are empty because of it. Homes and hands are empty because of it. It's been a journey of heartbreak, trials, and one that has taught me that whatever the outcome, we're in this together. He never faltered.

We always remember where we came from. Most of my childhood was a cinder block home with no central air and heat. I played out in the dirt, and on our ten acres, wild and free. I loved it. Cody and I come from humble beginnings, and we thank God daily for it. Each moment of raising our kids, we wonder how we will instill hard work, humility, and values of family, as we were taught. I love that he honors his past, acknowledging what needs to be changed, and is the change he wants to see in our life.

Caring for elderly and those that are unable to care for themselves is humbling and hard. Watching your spouse do that while being loving to those that can be unlovable is also very hard. I have seen Cody do this for so many. I remember the day that I realized the severity of the heartache that had been created in Cody's heart. This man cries when his heart breaks, but it is very rare and unusual. It makes me fall apart. Not physically, but in my heart.

People may seem cool, calm, and collected (as Cody), but we need to remember that many carry loads of the world within them. They need a little love and grace. Love them through it. I am aware that the heartache in my husband's heart is mine to help carry and journey with him as he navigates rough terrain. I did not believe that before, but with much reflection I have understood us to be one. The honor of walking alongside the rocky edges of life is one I cannot describe in words. It's something I pray about to help him carry the load. What a pure honor to walk alongside life with him. Sweet gentle giant.

Speaking of helping to carry a load. Cody has done that tenfold for me. Carrying the load of graduate school, as a high school principal, while having Irish Twins rocked our world. 2017 was a lot. High school principalship, getting accepted into the Cooperative Superintendency Program at The University of Texas in Austin, having both babies, selling and building a home was the year we will never forget. As I navigated those waters, I never felt alone. Cody was my rock. Cody is my rock. Cody was and is my island. He's my piece of solid ground, the one that I can lean on when the world comes crashing down. I am the ocean, he is my island, and I know he is staying right here. I learned this to be true through my doctoral work.

It was a strain, but it was also something that I didn't want to quit. We squeezed harder at the end, like toothpaste. We committed to finishing that program within two years so that the impact of our family was the outcome we wanted. WE did it. Oftentimes, I feel he deserves that doctorate far more than me. He is the stronghold of it. The core and yell leader of it. He is honestly one of the only reasons, along with our babies, I didn't quit. When you hear Dr. Lindsie Almquist, remember that Almquist has more to do with Cody than me. He was the true reason for the success. You cannot walk that journey of having babies, building a home, doctoral work, and principalship without a rockstar.

His impact on my life was highlighted during those years where he was selfless, a shoulder to cry on, and an amazing spouse. He reminded me one day when I felt overwhelmed by him being with our kids AGAIN by himself, "This is what we signed up for." He made it clear and articulated verbally that he wasn't babysitting or watching our kids. He was THEIR Daddy (even to the point that I kinda got a side eye when "Dad" was written on his Christmas stocking and not "Daddy"). He said as clear as day that he was doing what we signed up for and what he wanted to do as a Daddy. He gently reminded me that our children are NEVER a job, but instead our greatest blessings. It was an honor to spend time with them. Talk about stopping, dropping, and pivoting. He is the King of that. He knows and intentionally exhibits a positive difference in our lives, authentically and consistently. He never bats an eye at the real work of life: loving, caring, and being of strong virtue.

I remember getting a call about my best friend from middle school. Her husband had shot and killed her parents. I, to this day, still cannot believe it. Her brother is married to my cousin. My heart was pained for the reality these dear people had to face. As odd as this is, it rocked my world. I thought long and hard about the people in my life and how I needed to navigate my own emotions. These people were like second parents to me. They consoled me in my darkest hours as a child amid divorce and sadness. They treated me like their own in sweet Pettus, America (as everyone does there). I decided that I had deep wounds of pain that I needed to address. I called the Employee Assistance Program (EAP) in my school district and started therapy. Stop. Drop. Pivot. Teachers, staff, leaders, USE your EAP. It's OK.

I remember telling Cody about my pain. I thought he would dismiss my emotions since I had not been close to these dear friends for many moons. Instead, he loved me through it. Lots of tears. Drawers of pain I had closed were wide open, exposed like flesh after a bike ride gone south. Counseling impacted me far more than I thought it could. The impact of how my partner navigated all of that spilled over from it has been very influential. I learned about *Boundaries* by Dr. Cloud and Dr. Townsend. I use that book and talk about it to this day. I learned how to walk along with someone gently. To be a friend of courage and love, as Cody did for me. It's a big thing you can do for someone. Walk alongside them. Care more about their life than their situation. Ask about their current struggles and situations. Be okay with being muddy in the mess of life. Cody taught me that.

Cody is a behind-the-scenes, hard-working confidant. He is kind and gentle. Always, physically loving on me through the down days. We will be married ten years in February. He continues to show up. He stops, drops, and pivots. I am humbled and overjoyed that he is in my life, and that I have the privilege of being in his life. I will never take him for granted, that's for sure. He is the most influential person in my life. The impact of his life on mine has been so profound. When praying for the person I wanted to share with each of you, I chose him.

Mother Teresa said, "If you want to change the world, go home and love your family."

Cody exemplifies this. The world has absolutely been changed by him. I am honored to walk alongside him. His Pawpaw Gus, Dad, Uncle Gary, my Aubie, and Papa are watching down on him. His blessings will be out of this world.

Cody Leon, you're my favorite. You have made me be a better leader, "Lorax", and friend. The smallest things make the biggest difference. You have shown me that through and through. I remember that in the work I do for others. You exemplify a true friend and partner.

In all I do, I pray the individuals I am honored to serve, know that they have that in me. We're real. Life is messy. We forgive. We allow space to grow and learn through the trials and tribulations of life. It's a safe place. Through that arena I have been able to make a positive difference in this, oftentimes, very cruel world. The impact of your influence has forever changed me to be the wife, mom, leader, friend, and family member I am today. Thank you for being you.

ABOUT THE AUTHOR:

Social Media:
IG @lindsiealmquist
Twitter @servingkids
Email LindsieAlmquist@gmail.com

Lindsie is a passionate school leader in the central Texas area. She has served in public schools from elementary to high school as principal and at the central office. She loves traveling, spending time with family and friends, and volunteering. She is a proud Fightin' Texas Aggie, Texas State Bobcat, and UT at Austin Longhorn. She enjoys leading, learning, and being a part of the true work in this life: caring for our people.

DREAM IT, DO IT
Megan Marie Randall

It was a Wednesday night, I was laying back on the couch holding Drake, my dog. I was chatting, having deep, intellectual conversation with my close friend while contemplating my morning plans. Five days prior to this night, I had drove nine hours from El Paso to Austin. I stayed that night, then drove another three hours the next morning to Houston to celebrate my best friend's birthday. I left for Austin the next morning. I was originally planning to drive the nine hours back on Sunday night, but I didn't. I ended up staying three more days in Austin with my friend, spending some quality time out, catching up with others, and enjoying life. On this Wednesday night there was something in my gut and all over my body that was telling me it wasn't time to go back. I was missing something.

I know you are probably thinking, "Megan, it's called exhaustion. Of course, you didn't want to drive nine hours back!" That wasn't it.

I drive that route all the time. To be honest, it has become more like a regular comfort trip for me. A time where I can play my music, reflect, pray, and even plan my new ventures for upcoming goals. This feeling I was having, not being ready to go back, was different. It was like that feeling you get when you leave the house, but you know you forgot something, and you can't quit thinking about it or shake it off.

My friend and I were sitting there talking and sipping our tea. It finally dawned on me, I needed to do something I had never done before, that I had always wanted to do, something that scared me. Before I knew it, 30 minutes later, I was flushed, with uneven breathing, and had a flight booked in a few hours to New York.

She was looking at me in astonishment and asked, "Are you ok?" and then "Are you crazy?" when I told her what I had done.

I had no clean clothes, no hotel booked, no plans, and would be alone. I was scared, but I needed to do this. While I was on the couch telling her these things, I was also trying to narrow down for myself everything that scares me. I included some of my smaller dreams, the things that I said I would do someday, but never did yet, that made me smile. It took me several minutes until it struck me, and the lightbulb went off. Ever since I was younger, I had always dreamed of the day that I could just walk up to the airport counter, or get on my phone, and say, "Tell me where to go!" and then just do it.

I have always wanted to let go and be that spontaneous, fearless girl, since I have lived a life of complete control. When I say control, I am talking about my work schedule, feeling guilty when I'm not on the phone scheduling appointments. My body, eating and working out on a schedule. Feeling guilty if I have a night out. My internal people pleasing. Afraid to just be myself, worried about what someone is going to say about my words. Being the real me. I was so scared.

For someone who has lived a life of complete fear, people pleasing, and dominance over themselves, being spontaneous can be extremely difficult and terrifying. But deep down, something was telling me to be courageous and go for it.

Fast forward, I was at the airport, my heart was beating rapidly. There were so many chances for me to back out and cancel this trip ... but I didn't. Something deep inside was still telling me, "It's ok, keep going."

I arrived safely in New York and found a nice restaurant. I located an available seat at the bar, grabbed a glass of Pellegrino and Merlot, had a seat, and took a few deep breaths. I then begin to tell myself "Ok, we have nothing but time, so let's try something new."

I got on my phone and started searching. I ended up booking an AirBnB on the beach and a helicopter ride over the city. I took another deep breath and asked myself "What am I doing? Can I afford this? Will I be safe? Who will be with me?"

All these limiting belief questions were repeating over and over. It almost caused me to sabotage my own dream and go back home, but then, I looked up. I started to hear, "Megan, please just calm down. It's ok. You are ok. You have the money, the time, and the power. Just do it!" I carried on researching places and opportunities that made me smile. Then I put a game plan together.

During this journey, I had accomplished a few things on my bucket list that, surprisingly enough, I didn't think I would do. Believe it or not, I had the most incredible and amazing escape! I met so many great people. I was able to book the best AirBnB location. I had the greatest host I could have asked for on the beach, along with a cute puppy for a warm welcome! The lightbulb went off for me again, after I put down my luggage. Dean Graziosi was in my ear on his podcast, reminding me "Everyone's success looks different."

I looked around and realized he was right! This was a success for me, and a tiny step closer towards another achievement of mine. No one else's, but mine! I was free to do whatever I wanted! I could work. I could play. I could sleep. I could do anything without asking for anyone's permission! This was my time, my life, and it was a beautiful day! First thing that came to mind was food, music, and water! I asked my host if they had a bike. They did, and they let me borrow it! I rode that rusty bike all up the Long Beach boardwalk during sunset. I watched a full moon hover over the ocean. I stopped for some ice cream and wine that evening, all while playing my music. I had an amazing helicopter ride the following night flying over Yankee Stadium during a game. I even had an amazing time on the beach with surfers, waves, and really soaked in the beach life in the Northern Atlantic!

I literally lived a dream of mine. This wouldn't have happened if I kept trying to self-sabotage and talk myself out of it by making excuses for why I shouldn't go on this trip.

The next day after arriving to Austin from New York and then driving those nine hours home, I woke up early with energy. I got two incredible workouts in and got in my car ready to have an amazing Monday. Suddenly, my phone started to ring.

Marguerite's (a close, dear friend of mine) husband's name is scrolling across my screen. My heart stopped. I made myself push the answer button and said nervously, "hello".

I heard his tears, as he told me grievously, that Marguerite had passed the previous night. My heart stopped for a moment and everything around me froze. Tears begin to uncontrollably flow from my eyes. I began to weep so hard that I fell forward and attempted to hold my hand over my scream.

Marguerite and I met nine years prior in the small little town of Alpine, Texas. We were both two young, hopeful girls trying our best to live and make it in this crazy world. We had both just started our new jobs. I had nowhere to live besides my car and she stayed with family. We met every day for a while. We would discuss things we wished we had, things we wished we had done, and things we were determined to make happen. If I made a sale for work back in those days, I knew a few days later I would have money to book a room at the cheapest motel in town, to sleep in a bed. Twenty-year-old Marguerite knew my situation and did the most amazing act of service for me, she said she trusted me. She signed up to be a client of mine a week later. She also gave me a place to stay, and a new friendship built on trust.

She would confidently start every day by talking about her goals and needs, but then would always end with "I just gotta do it and have faith!"

We continued to be friends for many years to follow. She had fulfilled some of her dreams, such as getting married to the love of her life and having two beautiful children. Unfortunately, she was also struck with cancer.

Marguerite was positive, humorous, graceful, and determined. She did everything in her life with a smile and a huge loving heart, no matter who, or what it was she came across.

Later that day of hearing the news of her passing, in the middle of writing in my journal and crying, it finally dawned on me. The real reason that spontaneous trip happened was because of her!

She was the voice in my head saying, "Megan it's ok, just do it!" Because every time we spoke that's what she would tell me when we talked about our dreams.

Marguerite inspired and impacted me so much. The simple fact that though she was battling a severe cancer diagnosis, she was determined to live her best life, come hell or high water! She was determined to find love, get married, have kids, have fun, and help others. She absolutely did just that, without anyone's permission.

I'm dedicating this piece not just to Marguerite, but Nick, his mama Nicole, Dell, Jason, Esther, Darnald, and many other clients and friends of mine.

You see, sales has not just been about the money for me. Yes, it helps put a roof over my head. I have also been impacted and influenced so deeply from all these people's life stories in so many ways throughout the years. It has helped me become who I am today. In sales I have had an opportunity to fill more than a need with a product. I've been able to fill a need within my own heart, and that's my relationships.

You only get one life to live, and it's not even that long! You need to live every single day the best that you can. With no regrets! As long as you're not doing something illegal, just do your best, and let God handle the rest! You must have trust and have faith in Him that you will be ok. Remember, things are always happening FOR you and not TO you! Even if it's small things like a fender bender. Coffee spilled on your new pants. The relationship that didn't work. When you didn't get the job. Maybe you had an amazing record week at work. You accomplished your weight goal. You found your true love. You are getting a chance to learn how to control your attitude and becoming a better version of you every single day!

You have to wake up every morning and remind yourself that even if something bad or ugly happens that you didn't plan for, deep inside you know it will be ok! If a young boy is fighting for his life with cancer and can still smile and see the good in every day, why can't you? If a woman who lost all her hair from medications can still smile and see how pretty she is every day, why can't you? I have learned all this from reading and from all these influences I can proudly call friends of mine!

The only two things we truly can control each day, are our attitudes and our efforts. Like Marguerite told me all the time, quit holding yourself back from your dreams and just do it! During that journey if something happens, just hold still, and stop where you are. Put one hand on your heart and one hand on your belly. Take a long deep breathe, now exhale slowly, force a smirk on your face or you can smile. Throw on your favorite song, maybe some Bruno Mars, readjust the game plan, and keep going!

Again, you never know who you will meet or even run into during these tough times. You may, and more than likely will, end up meeting someone that will eventually impact or influence you in a way you never thought would happen. But how will you know if you don't go out there and try?

Take that trip! Do the workout! Take that job! Do the thing that you've been wanting to do! Everyone's success looks different so don't compare yours to anyone else's or ask permission! Put a little more trust and value in yourself today. Just do it and live your best life! You will impact and influence everyone else around you, because they will be watching you living your best life and want some of those vibes!

Xoxo,
Megan Marie

ABOUT THE AUTHOR:

Social Media:
IG @BluEyezz0124
FB @MeganMarieRandall
Email MM@MeganMarieEntity.com

Megan Marie has been an insurance agent for 10 years now with the company she represents. She has won many awards and broken records during her journey with the company. For any insurance questions or if you are interested in being hired, contact her. She'd love to help you get where you want to be and cover you at a time of need.

She is the CEO of Megan Marie Entity which it focuses on health and wellness. She is currently in the process of building her podcast, affiliate marketing, and merchandise among other things. Her mission is to share her story, educate others about the possibility of success, and help others implement the strategies so they can reach their definition of success!

Megan is passionate about helping and serving others. Her purpose in life is to constantly grow towards a crescendo of her own happiness. She's active with her city's Chamber of Commerce. Megan loves music, traveling, reading, and her dog, Drake. She's an Aquarius that loves being near water and creating. Her free spirit comes out of her like an eagle flying in the wind!

Website:
www.MeganMarieEntity.com

THE IMPACT OF LANGUAGE
Melahni Ake

I once heard a quote that said, "if you want to hire an expert to get a job done, hire a teenager while they still know everything." I used to chuckle every time I heard this quote. I was a teenager the first time I heard it. I imagine the first person that ever said this was a parent, friend, family member, or employer experiencing a challenging time communicating value with their teenager.

As we get older, we tend to see the world differently than when we were teenagers! We begin to understand that our language begins developing from the time we are born. We begin to understand the everyday responsibility of our choices that contributes to developing ourselves. We realize our language is a product of our beliefs and our beliefs affect our ability to make an impact in the world.

As a returning contributing author of the Impact of Influence, I am grateful to be included in this project with my friend Chip Baker. If you'd like to learn more about our history and Chip's impact on my life, pick up a copy of *The Impact of Influence Vol 3: Ladies Using Their Influence to Make an Impact*. Today, I'd like to share my journey with you about the impact of language, and how it has shaped my life.

When you think of my opening quote about teenagers and connect the dots to your own life, did you ever feel invincible, like a teenager that knows everything? I know I did. Dr. John Maxwell taught all the John Maxwell Certified Team Members at a conference one year and said, "I knew everything there was to know on how to be a parent until I became one."

I treasure every moment of learning from a mentor like John Maxwell. Choosing a mentor to learn from is not to be taken lightly, especially in this "social media frenzy world."

A mentor relationship:
- Adds Value to Your Life
- Helps You Become Aware of Where You Need to Grow
- Encourages You in Areas You Need to Grow
- Provides Ideas or Access to Resources to Help You Grow

I encourage you to make a list of things that are vital for you. What can you learn from your mentor that will positively impact your growth? Remember you also need to be very clear about WHY this mentor is essential to you.

I'll share the most important attributes of my relationship with John Maxwell as my mentor.

- Biblically Centered
- Credible
- Committed to Self-Improvement
- Visionary
- Inspirational
- Chooses Intelligent Language Over Sensationalism

John, as a mentor, tells you what he's learned. His ah-ha moments. His lessons from his failures. Most importantly, he inspires you because he shares his beliefs about leadership and the value of personal development in our lives.

I learned at the tender age of fifty-four that you always think you know everything about your situation until you learn more. You realize you have a lot more to learn when you learn more. When you open your heart fully to receiving, you open your ears to listening and understanding the value of serving others. When you open your heart to serving, you are on your way to becoming a humble servant leader.

Do you ever remember thinking you knew all the answers? What was it that gave you your "edge of confidence"? What did you enjoy doing in school? Did studying come easy for you? Were you a student-athlete? Were you a musician? Was it your circle of friends that gave you confidence? Was it volunteering in your community? Was it your sense of belonging to an established family name? Your older siblings? Is there a person you are grateful for helping you build your confidence?

As a believer, I am learning spiritual reflection's value and power. My early foundational years were critical times that helped me learn about survival strategy and how to overcome everyday obstacles that are outside of our control. My reflection is teaching me that what we experience allows us to validate our beliefs. Our evaluated reflection helps us recognize our triggers, our growth, and how we act.

I believe we all have the invitation to feel invincible and confident in our lives, because of the promise of everlasting life. I believe our confidence comes from knowing that we are enough in this world and are surrounded by GOD's love. I believe our intentional experiences and environment become a catalyst that influences the impact that we can make in the world. I believe in the biblical language that gives me confidence every day.

Jeremiah 1:5 says, "Before I formed you in the womb, I knew you, and before you were born, I consecrated you: I appointed you a prophet to the nations."

God's got this. There is no reason to feel insecure, intimidated, or unworthy. We were all designed to be uniquely perfect.

As early as I can remember, my mom, Joyce Brown, was one of the biggest influencers in my life, helping me to build my confidence. She was twenty-five when I was born and just thirty years old when she became a widow without a life insurance policy. In the summer of 1973, my father was diagnosed with lung cancer at twenty-nine years old and received treatment at Stanford University. We moved back to my grandparents' house in Orlando, where he only lived for a few months after his thirtieth birthday and died December 15, 1973.

I imagine my mom was just numb to the world at that time, accepted the responsibility, and moved through this transition with grace and determination. I remember her telling me recently that when we moved back to Indianapolis from Orlando, she just went back to work at the hospital like usual. She never told anyone that my father had passed away.

She said, "there were no other 30-year-old widows, no support groups, so I didn't talk about it. My friends at work just thought my husband was sick, and I didn't tell them anything any different."

Have you ever felt a need to do more? This impact was of isolation because there was no language or dialogue to support her. There were no cell phones, social media groups, classes, or community programs. When she told me the details of this time in our lives just a few years ago, I was heartbroken for her because I knew the rest of her life story. She didn't have anyone to confide in. She did this ALONE. The biggest lesson this has taught me is that it is all about our mindset. I've witnessed it. We can accomplish anything when there is no other choice.

Can you imagine going through a traumatic loss of a spouse and feeling like you have no one you can talk to about it?

COVID happened to the whole world simultaneously, yet can you imagine going through COVID without zoom, support groups, cell phones, and no one to talk to?

Can you imagine the impact of true isolation if you were the only one to go through it?

Can you imagine living in the world but feeling like you are just walking through it as a dream to survive?

Have you ever had an isolating experience like this in your life? How did you survive? Did you have a support system? What strategies did you use that you had learned from previous experiences? Did you change anything about your healing process? What approach would you teach someone else?

I gained my confidence by watching my mom go through challenging times. At five years old, I didn't know any of the details or the "grown-up decisions." Decisions like figuring out how to plan for before-work childcare. Mom had a Kinder-care worker who allowed me to be dropped off at her house before school started so my mom could get to work on time. To know how to budget for enough gasoline to get to work and back for the entire week. She had to buy enough groceries. She planned to have a safe place to live and pay rent at our apartment every month. I knew I could count on her; she always had a plan. She taught me survival skills.

In 1975, I was seven years old. I was attending a local elementary school on the south side of Indianapolis, and announcements were sent home at the end of the week. That week, the information was that HOCKEY registrations would be open that coming Saturday morning. I said I was interested in learning this, and my mom said, let's go check it out. We showed up at the address at the local PERRY PARK, and realized that it was ICE HOCKEY, not field hockey, as my mom had thought! The ice rink was an outdoor rink with a central fireplace (more like a fire pit these days), with dropped-down curtains, to protect the rink from the winter wind.

We looked around, and she said, well, what do you want to do? You can learn how to ice skate. Want to try it? The impact of this question changed my life. I said yes, and the rest is history.

What if my mom would have just said, "Oh, there is no way you can learn this. You don't know how to skate, and we don't have the money to pay for this?"

She didn't put any limiting beliefs in her mind or mine. She said, "Let's do it!"

She was excited for me to get on the ice. She helped me, after our practices, get to the fireplace to warm my skates up so we could loosen my laces. She had the heart to provide joy to her child. I believe her mindset was that this would be a time for us to build a new memory together.

We get stuck during the most challenging times in our lives. It's these times that we must look for new ways that push us outside our comfort zone and help us to experience a new path. Sometimes we need to permit ourselves to grow away from pain.

As a single parent, she figured out a way for us to buy hundreds of dollars of used equipment and budgeted for me to participate in one of the most expensive sports you can play. Ice time for Ice Hockey is costly. Ice Hockey is not like basketball, volleyball, track, or softball. All those sports have limited costs compared to ice hockey. I was the only girl in the all-boys league for over 12 years. Even as an only child, I ended up being blessed with a league full of "pseudo brothers."

This experience allowed me to learn many skills I needed for my life. The game of Ice Hockey is all about strategy. I loved it. I couldn't get enough of it. I felt like the time on the ice gave me a space that I couldn't get anywhere else in my life. I couldn't wait to go to practice and participate in our games every week. I give all the credit to my mom, Joyce Brown, for influencing my professional journey.

Ice hockey is about knowing the rules and seizing opportunities. My position was right defense, which meant I protected the zones, guarded my goalie, dug for the puck in the corners, and set up the play. This mindset allowed me to become an expert in strategic thinking. I had to make snap decisions that affected my entire line on the ice. It wasn't just about me; it was about my team's success.

This was a time when I began practicing the principles of servant leadership. What did I see in front of me? When was the right time to pass, protect, or shoot the puck? When was the right time on a power play to pull our goalie, to allow an extra player on the ice? When was the right moment to take the slap shot from the blue line? The speed of the game helped me to become a proficient problem solver. What kind of exercises do you do to improve your mindset?

I believe that this confidence is how many young adults see the world. Absorbing experiences for the first time causes a sense of self-righteousness, ego, pride, entitlement, or a self-centered reassurance. Athletes often describe this as an endorphin rush or a constant dose of adrenaline. Combine a developing teenager with an attitude of confidence, plus hormonal changes, and watch out, world.

In our teenage years, researchers say that our brain is still developing until age twenty-five. It is incredible to think that during these years, we are making choices that will impact the rest of our lives. Do you believe this?

I want you to stop right now and write down the answer to the following questions and think about all the decisions you made before the age of twenty-five.

Did you choose to further your education? Did you decide to get married? Did you choose to have children? Did you choose to serve in the military? Did you decide to become an entrepreneur?

Even though our brain is not yet fully developed, this time in our life represents these four critical areas that build or destroy our confidence.

1. Our beliefs about ourselves
2. What other people see in us
3. Our value in the world
4. Our ability to achieve success

I believe confidence at any age comes from your ability to grow your beliefs from your heart.

To become servant leaders, we must prepare our hearts daily for the language we use with ourselves and others. Our beliefs create our language, and our language controls our impact.

If you genuinely want to make a more significant impact in the world, think about the language you are using to influence others. Become intentional about where you give your time. Know your capacity for growth. Stretch your beliefs. Focus on Value. Become intentional about removing yourself from influences that no longer serve you. Believe in people. Become a bridge for collaboration. Learn to love helping people. Save space in your heart every day to love yourself. Fill Your Cup. Share your heart and create significance. Your biggest growth in life will come when you learn to meet others where they are every day.

ABOUT THE AUTHOR:

Social Media:
IG @everydayleaders50in50
FB @groups/everydayleaderswithmelahniake
Email Make@everydayleaders.com

Melahni Ake is the founder of Everyday Leaders Professional Coaching and Consulting. For 25 years she was a proven leader in Medical Device Sales, Training and Culture Development using her own training from Walt Disney World to challenge industries to create customer experiences that make a bigger impact in delivering value. She graduated with honors from the University of Indianapolis in Business Management and Organizational Leadership is a John Maxwell Team Certified Leadership Coach, Speaker and Trainer, eSpeakers International, and is a Certified Consultant with the WHY Institute. She's a 5 X Best Selling Author, Creator and host of Everyday Leaders Podcast in its 6th year, Leader of Everyday Leaders Morning Leadership Devotionals, Active Member of AWBO (Association of Women's Business Owners), Program Development for Top Floor Women- Indy's Premier Southside Women's Networking Group, Legacy Leader and Host of the Torch Talk Podcast for Pass The Torch for Women Foundation and Board Member of PTREA (Perry Township Religious Education Association). She is the Co-Founder of SCALE for Women, LLP.

Website:
www.everydayleaders.com

A LIFE-DEFINING MOMENT
Petra Krebbs

There are moments in your life that change your core. It is as if you shift from living life knowing who you are, to suddenly looking for yourself. There is a shift in your innermost being. You can't quite pinpoint it, but you know something inside of you is changing.

This is a life-defining moment and it creates a great impact. We will have many in our lifetime, but the first life-defining moment usually holds the greatest influence.

My shift happened as a young girl. I found myself walking around with my head down and my arms crossed. On the inside I was sad and angry. I was mourning a loss and resisting a change. I didn't lose a loved one, but maybe in a way I did. I am a first-generation immigrant. My parents left our home country to follow their dream and live a different life. For me it wasn't a dream, it felt more like a nightmare. Everything and everyone I knew, including the language I spoke was gone. I was twelve. I felt lost at an age where you are already trying to find yourself in your own backyard. Now I was Four thousand eight hundred and eighty-two miles away from anything that seemed familiar.

This kind of life-defining moment can happen in your own backyard too. *It is the shift from living life knowing who you are to suddenly looking for yourself.* Sometimes you push yourself to make a big life change, like my parents did. Even though you feel lost, it is exciting, because it was your choice to make the change, create a new life or a new self!

Most of the time these life-defining moments feel like they are not your choice. It feels like they are pushing you instead. They push you so far outside of your comfort zone that you fail to recognize your surroundings. It feels like you are lost, and you have no choice in the matter. Yet, I have learned that you do.

They call it a life-defining moment because we can choose how we allow this moment to impact and influence our life. This 12-year-old girl chose a posture of anger and sadness. I was very good at this posture by the way. I just wanted to be invisible. I begged my mom to buy me all the right clothes that everyone else was wearing and prayed every day, sometimes every hour of the day, to just blend in. "Dear God, please make me invisible. Please don't let anyone talk to me or look at me. Please stop the stares and the whispers. Please take me home."

No matter the effort, and the painful ways I tried to blend in, I just seemed to stand out. When you are walking around angry and sad with your arms crossed and your head down, and you are not able to speak the language, or understand anyone when spoken to, you tend to stand out.

My core was changing. I felt a giant shift, deep inside. I felt so far away from who I was. Most of all, my choices were shifting me into someone I didn't like. I could continue to keep losing myself in this shift or I could try another way. I wasn't sure what it would be, but it had to be better than this. At that age, I didn't know much about choices. I didn't know about mindset or the psychology of thought. I didn't have any mentors and I was not reading any influential books like this one. I felt very alone and lost.

Neale Donald Walsch said, "life begins outside of your comfort zone."

I would say that life's most important choices and lessons happen outside of your comfort zone. I was about to learn lessons that still influence my life today.

Does any of this sound familiar to you? Have you ever found yourself lost from a life-defining moment? Maybe like me, you allowed your circumstances to weaken your core? Many times, these moments are not your choice. You would rather be anywhere else. You rationalize your anger and sadness like I did. Yet deep down you know this is not making anything better. Maybe you are in such a life-defining moment right now.

Oh, how I wish we were sitting together with a cup of coffee, right now. (I am German, so I love my Kaffee!) Let's pretend we are, as I share some of my story and leave you with some thoughts for yourself. I hope what I share will ignite that powerful impact of influence of your own story.

Let's begin with a definition because I refer to this word a lot. The word core. The Webster Dictionary defines core /kôr/ as the central or most important part of something or the center of a fruit containing the seeds. It is often referred to as keeping something strong and stable. A negative impact on the core can cause a decline of strength and stability. A positive impact on the core creates sustained strength and stability.

My first life-defining moment was quickly creating a negative impact on my core. My strength and stability were declining. I put the blame on my circumstance, on everyone and everything else. Of course, it could not be my fault because it wasn't my choice. I did not choose to leave my country, my extended family, and my best friend. After several months of this negative impact, I realized my circumstances may not have been my choice, but I had to make a choice.

I could continue to blame everything out of my control, but none of those things were going to change. Or I could look at what I could control, me. When my world got quiet and I was forced to search myself, I found a few things. My attitude and my thoughts could be more positive. My behaviors could use some adjustment. Most of all, I wanted to feel like myself again. What if I took all those big, giant things that I couldn't change and set them to the side of my path, instead of continuously tripping over them? I was continuously arguing with myself. It probably wouldn't matter much because after all, the circumstance was out of my control. But I was just looking for a little difference. It turns out that the little turned into much. In the end, the little became everything. Every little thought and every little action you take flows out of your core into your circumstance.

I still didn't speak the language. I wondered how I could make any change at all when I couldn't communicate. How could I connect with anyone? I started to focus on what I could do instead of focusing on what I couldn't do. I took baby steps. I took 3 core steps that made a positive impact in that life-defining moment for me. They are steps I still take today, many years later. If you are in a life-defining moment maybe you can begin here.

3 Positive Impact Steps

Step 1: Uncross your arms
Step 2: Lift your head
Step 3: Add a smile

I began by changing my posture. I uncrossed my arms and lifted my head. Then I slowly added a smile. I always loved to smile, and I had forgotten how good a smile felt. You can feel a smile deep down into your core. I know, you are probably smiling now because these steps seem so simple. Yes, body language is a common language that we all speak. However, when you feel the most lost, when your life-defining moment is happening to you, and it is not your choice, these 3 core steps can be the hardest to choose.

Everything in you will want to do the opposite. Everything in you will pray to blend in and become invisible again. This is when you must remember the choice to protect your core. Don't allow the shift to take you too far away. Start with these simple steps when you feel the negative impact coming on. When you find yourself going down a negative path, focus on the smallest thing you can control. Maybe it is just uncrossing your arms or lifting your head.

I hope eventually you learn to add your smile. I learned that when you take an open posture to life, hope will find you.

Over time, I added other steps. I learned English. I made incredible friendships. I made this country my new home. I became hopeful to my core. People began asking if I was always this happy. They would ask why I didn't have any bad days. This shocked me. Of course, I do. If they only knew. Sometimes there are moments every day that make me want to cross my arms, hang my head, and take the path of anger and sadness. But I have already lived there. When you have experienced the silence and solitude of digging to the core of who you are, you learn that you need to protect it. You learn that you must make choices that will have a positive impact not a negative one.

You either withdraw from who you are with a negative impact to your core, or you deposit into who you will be with a positive impact. Since that first life-defining moment, there have been many others in my life. I also know there will be many more to come. Each of those moments have become opportunities for me to make deposits instead of withdrawals. My hope is that I will continue to become stronger and more stable. When you experience the power of positive impact on your life-defining moments, especially the challenging ones, it becomes your only choice. I will always choose hope.

The impact of influence is created by your choices. Your choices influence you and you will impact and influence others. My greatest hope is to help others find their strength in their life-defining moments. I have had the privilege to lead, mentor, and coach many in my corporate career, and as an entrepreneur. I love helping others discover how they are uniquely and wonderfully made. Many people spend their entire life trying to blend in like I did. We hide our stories; we diminish our gifts, and we compare our worth.

This reminds me of the game hide and seek. When toddlers play hide and seek, some will hide in plain sight and just cover their eyes. They think you can't see them because they can't see you. They want to blend in and be invisible. They even feel invisible, but they are seen. It is the same way for you. No amount of hanging your head or crossing your arms will make you invisible. You are seen and you are meant to be seen. You have a choice every day to make a positive impact for yourself and for others.

3Ps for a Positive Life

Those first three steps developed three other impact areas in my life. It wasn't until I was asked about my journey, that I even realized how important these areas are for me. They help me choose the positive impact path because it will not always be easy. It is certainly never easy in difficult times. The three areas of impact that I will share with you have been a constant intention and help to me personally and professionally. All three areas will shape the core of who you are. I call them my **3 Ps for a more Positive Life**.

#1 People: The Motivational Speaker Jim Rohn said, "You are the Top five people you surround yourself with." With today's influx of information, you are not only influenced by the Top five people you surround yourself with, but you are influenced by everything they are surrounded with.

One of the biggest gifts in my life has been the amazing people I have met. I have found that I am naturally drawn to people who are also choosing hope. I am inspired by people who work hard at creating a positive impact of influence in this lifetime. I would not be who I am today, or on the path that I am on, without the constant support and belief of my core people. I believe we are all better together.

When I started my teaching career, I sought out the teachers who focused on the things they could control instead of all the things that were outside of their control. And when I chose a new career in Direct Sales, I looked for others who chose hope. We kept our eyes on our purpose and encouraged each other along the way.

Even the twelve-year-old me found a small core group of friends that invested in getting to know each other better. They were patient, laughed with me, not at me, and encouraged me to keep going, and to keep growing.

Do you have your core people of influence? Are they having a positive impact on you? Maybe you don't have your Top five yet and you are still looking for them personally or professionally. I want to tell you a secret, they are also looking for you! You will find each other when you stay true to your core. Be sure to choose people who speak life and truth to you. Invest in people who have your best interest at heart, and you have the best for them. It takes intention and investment. It will be worth it.

#2 Power: Every powerful device you own needs to be plugged in, in order to power up. It is the same for you. You need to charge and recharge in all areas of your life. The energy you bring to this world begins at your core. There are too many people running on empty. I have been one of them and learned this the hard way. There are many different sources of power you can plug into. Are you plugging into things that bring you energy or drain you? Are you plugging into the things that are good for you? What gives you energy and makes you come alive? It is important that you take inventory of how you spend your time and what you give your energy to. Make a list and add or subtract power sources from your life according to your needs. You want to be fully charged to create your positive impact in your personal and professional life

My ultimate power source is my faith. God met me in that first life-defining moment. He took me out of the anger and the sadness of that circumstance. My faith my seed. It is my core. I am grateful for the source of His power above all else. This is where I plug in first. What is it for you? What is your ultimate power source? Start there.

#3 Practice: Practice makes progress not perfect! The path to creating a positive impact that is core deep and becoming your best self takes practice. Practice makes progress and it is progress that moves you forward. Your progress will create momentum. To keep your momentum, you need to keep moving every day, sometimes every hour of the day. What is something in your life that could use progress? Where do you need momentum? What could use more practice?

This twelve-year-old girl practiced uncrossing her arms, lifting her head, and adding a smile every day. I sat in the back of every classroom learning to read and write in a foreign language. There were days I didn't feel like it and days I wanted to give up. There were days I just wanted to go home. I am glad I didn't give up. That was a long time ago now, but the progress over perfection shaped who I am today. Continue your progress don't give up!

In closing, I would like for you to think about your own first life-defining moment. What is the impact of influence from that moment? It is your choice and I hope I get to hear it one day.

I need you to know something very important. In case you were wondering, you were never created to blend in. God created you to stand out! As your Strengths Strategist™, I know your unique talents are your strengths. They are needed to make a difference in this world. Our differences are our advantages. This book was created so that you would find strength from our stories because together we make this world a better place. Choose to define your moments instead of letting the moment define you!

ABOUT THE AUTHOR:

Social Media:
IG @petrakrebbs
FB @PetraKrebbsLLC
Email Petra@petrakrebbs.com

Petra Krebbs is a Speaker, Trainer and Coach for the Jon Gordon Companies and a Certified Gallup Strengths Coach. She is known as The Strengths Strategist™. She is passionate about engaging, equipping, and elevating others to achieve their best. Her energy is contagious and her focus on outcomes is refreshing.

Petra's professional career spans over 20 years in sales, leadership, training, and development where she helped organizations exceed their goals. She is an entrepreneurial thinker and led a thriving direct sales organization for over a decade. Jon Gordon's principles have been a guide in her personal and professional journey. Her experiences drive her passion to support others in their quest for excellence.

WILL IT TO BE
R-Jay Barsh

In a small basketball town nestled in the Pacific Northwest there once lived this sage of hoops and guru of all things mankind. His hometown was known for its incredible basketball teams and array of birds that flew with ferocious speed and freedom through the town. The town was an oasis for the guru. He had two unrelenting loves-basketball and birds. It has been said that the guru found a connection of strong will and creativity in a bird's flight, and an athlete's ascension to the rim.

When the sun came up in the morning all the townspeople knew they could find the humble guru unlocking the Towns Market, then crossing the street waiting patiently to teach the art of shooting the ball, or the patience in admiring the birds of the air. If the unassuming figure had an outdoor basketball court and a curious student, he had the ability to simplify life's most looming questions. Using the backdrop of nature and the outdoor court as a classroom he could, with a smile, a nod, and a basketball drill whisper life changing wisdom using simple basketball drills and encouragement.

His whispering wisdom would seep into the minds of those in his small town. Perhaps the location of the court played a role in the crowds that would gather since one could not visit the Town's Marketplace without seeing the guru shooting hoops across the street. Whether the guru had a crowd of one hundred or one, he always displayed a keen sense of teaching life through the game of basketball. However, when some of the Town's successful businessmen picked up the local paper from the Marketplace, they would snicker at the guru unlocking the door early in the morning, gently handing them a paper, then hovering around the court. They deemed it more of a distraction and an annoyance. The Town's Successful businessmen, some who became his biggest critics, didn't understand why crowds would gather to listen or sit with a man with no trophies that handed out newspapers. They didn't understand why the Guru was a favorite of the town's youth. He never won a Town Championship. He wasn't known as the best athlete, but without fail he handed out his newspapers with a smile. The basketball court was his classroom for life.

The critics had offices in the middle of town, full of trophies and plaques of achievements. Many people in the town knew the critics were successful. However, very few stopped by to admire what they had achieved, congratulate them on the letters of achievement, or the huge fish and wild game that painted the walls of their offices.

Simultaneously, the Guru known as Fredrick would often be found sitting near the outdoor courts watching and admiring the birds of the air, patiently waiting for the ball to bounce near his feet. His natural ability to be near the court and present with nature stirred the curiosity of the kids in the town. Often, the kids would ask the guru how to shoot the basketball better, or why he found the birds of the air to be so impressive. Every Spring, the community would take all the youth basketball teams, have the towns largest gathering, and crown the Town Champion Youth Team. Even though the Guru didn't coach a team in the Town, the Tournament always reminded the people of Fredrick's passion and purpose. This was seen as his court-classroom and his home. Year after year, the basketball tournament would culminate with a new champion on the court, but the same champion of wisdom reigned—the old guru. Players and coaches alike would be seeing high fiving and acknowledging the guru as the games were being played, it had become a tradition of sorts.

The old guru did not seek to be the end all be all. He simply decided daily to practice what he called PPR. **Purpose, Passion, and Responsibility**. The guru made a silent commitment to always be available to the youth of his small-town.

Purpose increases commitment, passion fuels connection, and responsibility cultivated accountability.

For fifty plus years, the town leaned on the guru to answer tough questions. With his calm presence, he never failed them. Fredrick believed a strong PPR is like having a high free-throw percentage. With daily repetition, anyone could hit the game winning free-throw, or pass the tough school exam. It was all about learning and the guru always said, "Repetition is the mother of all learning."

However, as time went on, a few of the town's critics, mainly Coach John the bird-catcher, began to become very frustrated. With all their business and Youth Coaching accomplishments no one saw them like they saw the Guru. John the bird-catcher and his buddies decided it was time for a new guru. To become the town's most coveted voices, they would have to embarrass the guru with a question he could not possibly answer.

One day while Coach John the bird-catcher and his buddies were preparing their number one ranked team for the big basketball tournament, they had a brilliant idea.

The Idea

When they won the Championship game in front of the entire town, they would take the moment to pose a question to the old guru, a question that he could not possibly answer. They excitedly began to feel the momentum of what it would be like to be the wisest coaches in the town. They fantasized about crowds running to their downtown luxurious offices and paying big fees to answer any life question they may have. They spoke about being on the front page of the town's newspaper. The critics of the guru knew that all eyes would be on them after a big win. In that moment, they could embarrass the guru so much he'd have to leave town.

After weeks of preparing on the court, they created the one question the guru could not answer. The critics said, "Let's go to the outdoor court where the guru watches birds. Before we win the championship, let's buy a few of the birds from the local pet store. When we are in front of the entire town, with all eyes on us with our championship trophy in one hand, we will all have a small bird in the other hand. We will yell to have the guru come answer a simple question. 'Guru in each of our hands we have a small bird. Since you know everything, we want to know ... Are the birds in our hands dead or alive?'"

The critics strategically decided that if Fredric the guru answered that the birds are alive, then they would take their thumbs and crush the birds. Then open their hands and prove the guru was wrong. If the guru said the birds are dead, they would open their hands. The entire town would see the birds fly away. The critics laughed and went on preparing their team for the big game. They couldn't wait for this massive moment.

The Spring arrived and the courts were alive with players competing. Everyone in town was closely watching to see if any team could beat the number one team coached by John the bird-catcher. After two days of competition, the Championship Game was on full display. In a back and forth battle the number one ranked team pulled away and won the Town's Championship. John the bird-catcher could sense people whispering about how great his team was. All he thought to himself was, "It is now time to embarrass the guru and become the wisest man in town."

As the crowd gathered to watch the ceremony of trophies, the moment had arrived. As John received his trophy, his buddies chuckled and yelled at the top of their lungs for the guru Fredric to come to the center of the court. With the joy of life, the guru jumped up and stood quietly. He had no idea about the plan that the critics had forged for him. It was now time to pressure the guru with the simple question.

John started the conversation, "Hey Guru, you waste all this time teaching about purpose and passion. You seem like the wisest man in the town. It's been said that YOU know everything. My buddies and I have a question."

At that moment, the buddies scurried behind John the bird-catcher all slightly clutching their hands.

The crowd was now anticipating what would happen next. All eyes were now on the Championship Coach, John the bird-catcher. He continued, "Guru in our hands we all have a bird. We want to know, are these Birds dead or Alive?"

The crowd had a great gasp and all heads turned to the direction of the Guru. With the fate of the bird's existence manipulatively woven into whatever he answered, the guru took three deep breaths and responded, "Coach John, the birds are what you WILL them to be. With anything in life, it is our WILL that decides the outcome. Our WILL shapes our existence. Whatever your intentions are you can at this time, Will it to Be."

At that moment, John and his buddies made eye contact. The crowd looked up with the guru and admired the three birds that flew away. The town erupted in cheer as the guru once again used the court as his classroom to teach the ultimate skill of will and intentions. The guru wasn't the wisest man in the town. He just remembered that when his Family gave him the keys to the marketplace, he never forgot that life is about the people we serve. He utilized the court across the street to honor that commitment. PPR

---Half man half amazing, the guru, Poppa, Suavador, Coach, Brother, friend whatever role Fredrick J. Crowell felt it was vital to fill in a person's life he embodied it fully. He did not seek to lead all people, but those who leaned in his direction, those who belonged to an unspoken tribe of neighborhood changers. Crossing through the complexities of religion and systematic boundaries his leadership principles were simple yet divinely profound. Although he used the basketball court as his pulpit, his message has reached

from the halls of politics to the rural Villages of Alaska. Let this story of Will remind us that it is our intentions that shape our lives.

"Look at the birds of the air; they neither sow nor reap nor gather into barns, and yet your heavenly Father feeds them...consider the lilies of the field, how they grow; they neither toil nor spin, yet I tell you, even Solomon in all his glory was not clothed like one of these."
-Sermon on the Mount

PPR.

ABOUT THE AUTHOR:

Social Media:
IG @coachrjaybarsh
Twitter @coachrjaybarsh
Email rbarshjr@gmail.com

R-Jay Barsh is a veteran with more than 15 years of coaching experience. He has been named an assistant basketball coach at Florida State by Head Coach Leonard Hamilton. Barsh was an assistant coach at Boise State the past three seasons where he helped lead the Broncos to the 2022 NCAA Tournament. While there, they set program records for total wins (27), conference wins (15), and consecutive wins (14), on their way to winning the Mountain West regular-season title outright and capturing the Mountain West Tournament championship.

Boise State became the fifth team in the history of the Mountain West Conference to win both the outright regular season championship and the conference tournament championship in the same season in 2022. Barsh was an assistant coach at Boise State in each of the past three seasons as the Broncos averaged 22.0 wins per season.

On the strength of its sensational season, Boise State earned a No. 8 seed in the 2022 NCAA Tournament.

Barsh also helped Boise State to the quarterfinals of the NIT in 2021.

Prior to his tenure at Boise State, Barsh spent the previous seven seasons as the head coach at Southeastern University in Lakeland, Fla. While with SEU, he led the Fire to three NAIA Division II National Tournament appearances, the first for the program in school history. In his second season, SEU went 27-7 and reached the NAIA Fab Four during its first postseason tournament run. Ultimately earning Barsh a nod as a finalist for the Don Meyer National Coach of the Year Award. Barsh also led the Fire to tournament appearances following the 2017-18 and 2018-19 seasons.

Barsh helped lead Tacoma Community College to three Western Region titles in four seasons and an NWAACC championship in 2012. The Titans also made the Elite 8 in the NWAACC Tournament in 2009. Prior to TCC, he spent one season at Lincoln High School (Tacoma), where he helped guide the school to the state's Final Four and a record of 26-5.

Barsh also served as an assistant coach at the University of Puget Sound, his alma mater, from 2005-07. In his first season with the Loggers, the program finished with a 26-5 mark and a NCAA D-III Elite Eight appearance.

Barsh played collegiately for TCC from 2001-03, where he helped lead the Titans to a record of 30-3 and an NWAACC title (2001-02). He was an all-conference honoree the following season.

GRIEF TO GREATER
TaMeka Martin

Influence is a powerful thing that every human being possesses. According to Yahoo dictionary online, "influence is defined as the capacity to have an effect on the character, development, or behavior of someone or something."

The influence one has on the world can be used to uplift or discourage. My calling every day of my life is to live on purpose, with purpose. Though I have faced many trials, I have also faced many triumphs. As a human being, we have the opportunity to face our days being bitter or being better. My hope is to choose the latter of the two, daily.

Born to teenage parents in May 1979, many would say that the cards were stacked against me before birth. However, my faith tells me that God didn't make a mistake when he formed me in my mother's womb. From the start I was destined to be here. I was created with a Divine purpose. Through nurturing from my family in the Christian Faith, I have grown through each season of my life. The Lord reveals and continues to expose my purpose.

As I reflect on the monumental moments that shaped the trajectory of my life, my journey with grief has been the foundation for my strength and determination to make my mark on the world. My grief journey started on August 15, 1985 in Calvert, Texas. As a six-year-old, this experience with the grief process began when I witnessed my three-year-old brother, Jamaal, get killed by a drunk driver in front of my older cousin and myself. This event laid the foundation of my faith and my focus.

As a Christian, my faith is what sustains me. My belief in the Word of God shapes the way I view every aspect of my life. I know that I would not be where I am if it wasn't for my faith in God and my belief in Jesus Christ as my Lord and Savior. Persistent, specific, and intentional prayer has always helped me to look at life and take the best attributes to help continue in the perpetuation of my purpose.

The pinnacle of my grief journey occurred on October 25, 2021, with the tragic death of my mother, Chere. My mother had celebrated her sixtieth birthday twenty days prior. The day before her transition, my daughters, Khloe and Kadence, my mother and myself had one of the best celebratory days of her life. We went to church and praised the Lord. We had brunch to celebrate the establishment of my new business endeavor, G.L.A.M. and Girlfriends, LLC. We celebrated her first professional basketball game experience by cheering on our Houston Rockets. As I dropped my mom off at her place of residence, we engaged in our normal parting salutations.

My mom, Chere' would never say goodbye. "See you later!", she exclaimed, "I love you!"

I exchanged similar words, not knowing that this would be the last conversation and the last time I would see my mother alive in her physical form. This experience has enlightened and continues to illuminate the rest of my physical existence on this earth.

Grief makes you analyze every second of every minute. Every minute of every hour. Every hour of every day. Grief teaches you that every moment matters. Grief encapsulates your thoughts. It helps in the evaluation of what really matters and why you were created. Grief is a journey that we will all face, not a destination we reach. It is a journey that begins and continues throughout your physical existence.

The lessons I have learned on this journey, as I use my God given gifts to make a positive impact on this world are:
- to live on purpose, with purpose
- to grieve and grind
- to mourn as I move.

Though they are simplistic in nature, these are the principles that make me who I am. They serve as the cornerstone for positioning myself for impact and influence. To impact and influence the world, you have to be in the trenches of life's journey. That impact is felt when you make big moves and have bold faith. When you are a change agent and help to influence change in others. When you become a hope dealer and not a delivery of despair.

Living on purpose, with purpose requires big moves and bold faith. What is faith? According to the Google dictionary definition, "Faith is complete trust or confidence in someone or something. It is a strong belief in God or the doctrine of a religion, based on spiritual apprehension rather than proof."

Hebrews 11: 1 (KJV) says, "Now faith is the substance of things hoped for, the evidence of things not seen."

Boldness requires self-confidence and self-awareness. Self-awareness is how clearly we see ourselves. This includes our values, passions, aspirations, thoughts, feelings, behaviors, strengths, and weaknesses, along with our impact on the lives of others. Being self-aware is a great quality and it helps in the process of understanding who you are. If you don't know who you are, or are not comfortable with who you are, how can you influence others?

We cannot change people. We can only influence change through walking the talk and leading by example. Influence through leadership starts with being a change agent. Change is one of the biggest, if not the biggest constant in our lives. Yet it is a challenging thing for many to face. Change is an aspect of human behavior. As humans and influencers of others, we know that human behavior can be unpredictable. Human behavior is at the heart of it all and many times is one of the most challenging factors to understand.

Northouse, P. (2016). Leadership: theory and practice (7th ed.). West Michigan University, USA: Sage. What factors in your daily walk and talk influences others around you to embody positive change?

Grief has allowed me to learn how to cherish and challenge myself in every moment while pushing myself and others towards their purpose. You can say I am a Purpose Pusher. My influence lies in helping others believe in the purpose of who they are and why they are created to be in the spaces they are placed in their life's journey. Being an agent of change is part of the grieving and grinding process. When one grieves, they suffer grief, they mourn. Grief is a response to loss. It starts internally and manifests externally. Grind as defined by Urbandictionary.com is, "Repetitive actions in order to make the character stronger or working hard."

Grieving and grinding requires you to take what is happening internally, that manifests itself externally, and transform negative energy to positive energy to produce positive, purposeful outcomes. When I lost my brother at such an early age, my grief initially became rage. Rage can be detrimental and destructive if it is not harnessed to be a driving factor in building a positive, productive life. This factor was quickly recognized by my family. I was taught to transfer those negative feelings into productive endeavors such as sports, church, and other social, civic, and volunteer activities. This was only accomplished through positive influencers in my life that modeled the benefits of positive change.

If negative feelings are left unresolved, it minimizes positive outcomes, and maximizes the chances for negative outcomes. All outcomes, both positive and negative, help to shape us into who we are purposed to be. If you are aligned in your purpose, your triumphs overshadow your trials. Your tests become the platform for your testimony. I have always had a gift of transforming my pain into purpose.

In 2020, I was called to lend my story, my testimony, to a Women's Global devotional, Promise - God's Assurance on the Cross for Our Crown. This opportunity awakened my passion to bring my influence to the world through my written words. My Promise Scripture is Galatians 6: 9 (NLT), "So let's not get tired of doing what is good. At just the right time we will reap a harvest of blessings if we don't give up."

Fast forward to November 2021, in my preparation to eulogize my mom. I wanted to impart words of inspiration to those who would help in the celebration of life for my mother. I reflected on that body of work and my continued journey in this world without the person who brought me into it, my mother. I know my mother would want me to make sure that I used that moment to continue to influence others, just like I had since before I was born. My mother always expressed to me that I saved her life. She knew that God had placed me in her womb, to do great works and provide great influence for His people. In this moment I had to grieve, grind, and mourn as I continued to move!

As I opened up to talk about my mom, I started with saying, "I will grieve my Moma until I go to the grave. My flesh is weak, but my spirit is strong, knowing she is resting in the Lord until we both reach our eternal home. Being together once more! I was in awe that while I was experiencing great physical sadness and pain, I also experienced true spiritual happiness and joy.

"I knew you before I formed you in your mother's womb, before you were born, I set you apart and appointed you as my prophet to the nations." (Jeremiah 1:5 NLT).

Who am I? How do I make a positive influence on the world? I am TaMeka DeAnn Chopp Martin. I am a Believer, Daughter, Sister, Wife, Mother, Niece, Friend, Soror, Trainer, Speaker, Innovator, Educator, Elevator, and Entrepreneur. I am a G.L.A.M. Girl. A Go-Getter, Leader, Advocator, and Motivator. I am the light in the darkness through Jesus Christ that lives within me. I am the product of teenage parents raised by a village of people who instilled greatness into me. It started with the legacy created by my grandparents, Alonzo and Jimmie Ray Chopp and coupled with the love of my mother, Chere Chopp-Flentroy, my daddy Charlie Ray Flentroy. My father who helped to create me, Charles Roach, Sr., my maternal Aunt Sheryl Chopp, my maternal Uncle's Willie Toles, Alonzo Chopp Jr., and James Ray Chopp, my brother Markus Miguel Flentroy and a host of other family and friends that helped pave the way!

    I have learned that if you keep moving, keep making things happen, and keep failing forward, nothing or no one can stop what God has purposed for you and your legacy. What sustains me and gives me the Earthly desire to mourn as I move is the legacy that I am creating with my husband, Gregory and our beautiful daughters, Khloe Alexandra (Blossoming Defender of Mankind) and Kadence Alyse (With Rhythm God is my Oath). As I lead a life of service and servant leadership through my church, job, businesses, as well as social and civic organizations, I live by this principle, "For I know the plans I have for you," says the Lord. "They are plans for good and not for disaster, to give you a future and a hope." (Jeremiah 29:11 NLT)

ABOUT THE AUTHOR:

Social Media:
IG @glamandgirlfriendsllc
FB @tamekachoppmartin
Email glamandgirlfriends2020@gmail.com

TaMeka C. Martin is a native of Bryan, Texas by way of Calvert, Texas. She graduated from Bryan High School in 1997. She received a Bachelor of Science in Electrical Engineering (2002), a Masters of Business Administration (2005) from Prairie View A&M University, and a Masters of Educational Administration (2011) from Lamar University. She is currently a Doctoral Candidate in the College of Education pursuing her studies in Organizational Leadership with an emphasis in Organizational Development from Grand Canyon University.

As an undergraduate at PVAMU, she received an academic and athletic Scholarship. She excelled in Track and Field, various organizations, and became a member of Alpha Kappa Alpha Sorority, Inc.

In 2003, she started her career in Public Education as a classroom teacher and coach in Conroe ISD. She also served as a classroom teacher in Klein ISD. She quickly excelled through the profession as a Math teacher, Math and Science Curriculum Coordinator, Math Instructional Specialist, and Programs Facilitator for Splendora ISD, and now as Assistant Principal at Splendora High School.

Being a lifelong learner, she pursued her dreams of entrepreneurship and received her Real Estate License from the Champions School of Real Estate in 2015. In 2017, she became a Real Estate Columnist for Houston Stylist Magazine. In 2020, she became a Published Author when she Co-Authored, Promise - Women's Global Devotional and in 2021 Contributing Author for I'm Speaking - Affirmations Legacy Edition.

Currently, she resides in Spring, Texas where she lives with her beautiful family, her husband Gregory (Greg), and two daughters, Khloe, 13 and Kadence, 8.

A life of service and servant leadership is what drives her as she serves through her church, job, businesses, as well as social and civic organizations.

Guiding Scripture
"Let us not become weary in doing good, for at the proper time we will reap a harvest if we do not give up."
-Galatians 6:9

THE POWER OF ONE
Victor Pisano

Life is meant to be experienced in the moments. Yet so often, we distance ourselves from that in-the-moment experience. We consciously (or sometimes even unconsciously) allow distractions to cloud our thoughts, ruminating over what yesterday held, and fretting over what tomorrow could be. In doing so, we are surrendering to that which we have no control over. In contrast, when you live where your feet are, the possibilities for true fulfillment are all around you. With a commitment toward open-mindedness along our journey, mindfully maintaining a genuine connection to what is happening in the moment, the path toward growth opens wide.

When we grow through the opportunities to experience the lessons from those around us, we are slowly being shaped into influential leaders. In turn, the hard-earned wisdom and insight we accumulate allows us to pay it forward, eliciting greatness in others as those we connected with have done for us.

Here's the thing, the power of influence will always be a part of our path through the people we choose to surround ourselves with. Depending on our choices, that can become our greatest strength, or our biggest regret. But with careful choices, I am telling you that the ability to become motivated and blossom, both personally and professionally, through the wisdom of others is entirely within your control.

Imagine a life where you are gifted with mentors to become who you were meant to be. Having the ability to make an impact on others and elicit the greatness they carry within them is fulfilling. I know this because I have been walking that path for quite a while. It's not always easy for us to have something that we are called to share with others. One must also keep their own cup filled. But during the times where I find myself questioning my influence or worth, I come back to the singular thing that drives me.

It's a simple philosophy…

As long as **ONE** person is listening, following, reading and/or being inspired, then I have done my job.

THIS IS THE POWER OF ONE.

It's a bit of a mind trick, really, because impacting a person is like throwing a pebble into the still surface of a pond. The ripples extend further and further outward, reaching shores in all direction. Similarly, if you can change the thought pattern and inspire or motivate just one person, imagine how many lives that one person can change during their own life. And here's the catch: you never know who that one person is.

> *"To the world, you might just be one person. But to that one person, you may be the world."*

Too many people think they are either unqualified or have missed their chance to be that one person. I'm here to tell you to stop the *"what ifs"*, *"I should haves"*, or *"if onlys"*. Those are excuses, not solutions; phrases that will only lead you down the path to regret as you get older. You're better than that — you can do great things. The journey will require patience, sacrifice, persistence, and self-awareness — but you have what it takes.

When you look around, do you ever see a world where...
- **People accept fear and quit**
- **People who try to challenge themselves can't get out of their comfort zone**
- **People with strategy have no passion**
- **Leaders don't have followers**

What a stagnant, colorless place to dwell. But this is precisely your chance to be the POWER OF ONE. You can make a difference. It starts with looking deep within yourself to discover the passion that will lead to your purpose. Be the impact, even if it starts under your own roof. Positivity and change are not defined by the numbers you affect, but rather the impact you make. We all start small, build the foundation, and, as long as we take small steps forward — we progress. By maintaining momentum and operating with integrity and character, we will experience growth. The circular ripples in the pond grow wider and wider.

I've been blessed to have so many people in my life willing to take the time to invest, inspire, motivate, and empower me to become successful. As a result, I want to pay it forward. It feels incredibly selfish to keep the lessons I have learned to myself. Instead, I view sharing them with others as my calling and privilege. These experiences that impacted my life, brought about by the genuine, authentic mentors I surrounded myself with, taught me the importance of individual growth. Along with the sometimes-painful lessons that come as we experience the challenges life places in front of us, the combined lessons learned drive growth for us and set the stage for powerful impact on others.

Growth is something we must pursue to remain healthy human beings. Stagnation is not in our nature — our culture is constantly evolving. We can find opportunities for growth in many areas of our life: personal, spiritual, in our relationship, and in our career. But the pursuit of growth comes with an important caveat.

I try to be realistic and often have to temper expectations. One of the unfortunate outcomes of the warp speed that today's technology brings is that far too often, we no longer respect the concept of process. We live in a society of instant gratification that has stripped us of the opportunities to develop our sense of patience — we simply don't have the skills required to wait. However, some things can't be rushed, nor were some things ever intended to be. The analogy I most associate this with is "Rome wasn't built in a day." Instead, it took time and strategy to create greatness.

"Patience is not simply the ability to wait — it's how we behave while we're waiting."
— Joyce Meyer

There is a fantastic, illuminating parable about the Chinese Bamboo Tree that I often talk about when explaining the importance of the lessons of growth through patience, faith, and perseverance. Similar to most other plants, the Chinese Bamboo Tree requires the proper conditions to thrive: ample water, fertile soil, and the right amount of sunlight. However, what is distinctly different about the Chinese Bamboo Tree is that one full year after planting, you will see no sprouting. A second year will pass, and still, there is no visible activity to observe. As the third year arrives, things look no different from those first two years. When the fourth year arrives with nothing to see yet again, one would expect despair, frustration, or anger from the farmer tending his plant. But to grow the Chinese Bamboo Tree, the farmer must be patient. That's because it's not until the fifth year that it seems like the miracle of growth begins, and in a radical way.

Remember, the farmer has nurtured this plant for five years. He's invested time, resources, money, and most of all, his patience in not rushing the outcome. And in choosing to respect the process, the rewards are incredible. That Chinese Bamboo Tree will grow up to 80 feet in six weeks! Numerous culms, or small hollow shoots, will grow in an entire field. Four years of being stagnant — only to epically flourish in the fifth year?

We tend to judge growth by what is visible and tangible, but not all growth shows outwardly. Growth typically occurs within before the results spill out onto those around us, or we need to call upon them. In other words, we may spend years developing a skill that is not necessarily required in our current environment. Still, we are building ourselves up for success in the future. Think about characteristics such as integrity, character, knowledge, faith, perseverance, and gratitude. These traits require the same nurturing process as the Chinese Bamboo Tree. That tree didn't lie dormant for four years; it did quite the opposite. Below the soil was an explosion of roots growing in width and depth, capable of supporting its outward growth once it was finally ready to sprout.

"Without patience, we will learn less in life. We will see less, and we will feel less. We will hear less. Ironically, rush and more usually mean less."
- Mother Theresa

The lesson within the lesson is that growth lies in the ability to be patient, and to trust what others — or even you — cannot yet see. When building your dreams, goals, and purpose, you must have the willingness to overcome the adversity, barriers, fear, and doubt that accompany the process.

Take a minute to imagine if the tree did grow rapidly after just one year. The first strong wind of the season would bring it down. It would have destroyed the potential to reach the impressive height that people see and admire in the fifth year. The Chinese Bamboo Tree requires a stable base of roots to sustain its height and weight. The same goes for each of us as we grow into the person we are meant to be. We need to trust the process and stay in the present to properly establish a sustainable foundation of roots.

This is where the impatient are tempted to look for shortcuts and excuses to portray a prepared and grounded person. But I guarantee that you will be unable to maintain the hollow confidence that you once started with. Remember, what we establish inwardly will eventually be exposed outwardly. If you live by the mantra, "Fake it until you make it," I have bad news...this approach is not strategy and is temporary at best. You cannot build anything of substance quickly or on top of shallow, shifting ground.

It's important to remember that personal growth is not necessarily something that comes naturally. It takes time, focus, and a deliberate commitment if we truly wish to better ourselves. It is a slow process; in some cases, you won't see the results for months or even years. But what you earn with that patience and effort is worth it in the long run. If you are willing to be persistent and accept the victories of small steps, I assure you the reward will far outweigh the investment. Too often, we see people who have allowed the growth process to frustrate them to the point that they want to move on to where "the grass is greener." Instead, think about the Chinese Bamboo Tree. The farmer didn't move on to the next thing, but instead, committed to making what he had greener — with tremendous reward.

Growth is not associated with luck — it is an outcome of becoming comfortable stepping outside your comfort zone with a passion to be the best you possible. Like growth, success is also a series of small steps forward. It isn't always leaps and bounds, although if that does occur, it is often a result of your commitment. In most cases, the objective is to keep moving forward, one foot at a time if that's what it takes.

It wouldn't be right to close without noting an essential element here is that is also at play. Sometimes, standing still actually results in moving forward, as long as you have paused for the right reasons. There are specific scenarios in life that for growth to occur, you must stop and evaluate the situation. That is still a conscious choice, thus I still consider this part of a forward-moving journey.

If you are committed to this growth process and respect the investment of time and patience, you will develop influential qualities. As a result, the work you have done will be reflected back to others who need it, whether you know it in that moment or not. And that is how you will experience the fulfillment provided by the **Power of One.**

Do great things today and make a difference.
Humbled to lead, Victor.

ABOUT THE AUTHOR:

Social Media:
IG @charge_up_today
FB @chargeuptoday
Email chargeup@satx.rr.com

Victor Pisano has inspired executives, entrepreneurs, leaders, high school and college student-athletes across the country with his leadership platform, Charge Up. At the core of its foundation is that leadership is both a gift and a privilege, and we must pay it forward and elicit the greatness in others to make a positive impact. To inspire and empower people who are willing to invest in their goals and push past the barriers so that they can discover their passion, find their purpose, and have the courage to act with integrity as they pursue their path to fulfillment. Speaking for over 20 years, he is also certified as a speaker and trainer through the John Maxwell Academy, Jon Gordon's "Power of a Positive Leader," and the Third Rivers, "Leading with Values" program. Visit him at www.chargeuptoday.com

ABOUT THE LEAD AUTHOR

Chip Baker is a fourth-generation educator. He has been a teacher and coach for over twenty-two years. He is a multiple-time best-selling author, YouTuber, podcaster, motivational speaker, and life coach.

Chip Baker is the creator of the YouTube channel and podcast *Chip Baker—The Success Chronicles*, where he interviews people from all walks of life and shares their stories for positive inspiration and motivation.

Live. Learn. Serve. Inspire. Go get it!

Email: chipbakertsc@gmail.com
Online Store:
http://chip-baker-the-success-chronicles.square.site/
Facebook Page:
https://www.facebook.com/profile.php?id=100014641035295
Instagram: @chipbakertsc
LinkedIn:
http://linkedin.com/in/chip-baker-thesuccesschronicles-825887161
Twitter: @chipbaker19

Chip Baker—The Success Chronicles

YouTube: youtube.com/c/ChipBakerTheSuccessChronicles
Podcast: https://anchor.fm/chip-baker

Other Books:
Growing Through Your Go Through
Effective Conversation to Ignite Relationships
Suited for Success, Vol. 2
The Formula Chart for Life
The Impact of Influence Vol. 1,2, 3, & 4
R.O.C.K. Solid
Stay on the Right Path
Black Men Love
The Winning Mindset
Concrete Connections

PICK UP THESE OTHER TITLES BY CHIP BAKER

 GROWING THROUGH YOUR GO THROUGH

 EFFECTIVE CONVERSATION TO IGNITE RELATIONSHIP

 SUITED FOR SUCCESS: VOLUME 2

 THE FORMULA CHART FOR LIFE

 THE IMPACT OF INFLUENCE: VOLUME 1

 THE IMPACT OF INFLUENCE: VOLUME 2

 R.O.C.K. SOLID

 STAY ON THE RIGHT P.A.T.H.

 THE IMPACT OF INFLUENCE: VOLUME 3

 BLACK MEN LOVE

 THE IMPACT OF INFLUENCE: VOLUME 4

 THE WINNING MINDSET

To order your autographed copies visit
http://chip-baker-the-success-chronicles.square.site/